CHASING *Wildlife* SECRETS

Praise for *Chasing Wildife Secrets*

"Scott McCorquodale isn't just a wildlife researcher by profession. He was born hardwired with uncommon curiosity about wild creatures, and the developed skills, drive, and grit to discover and learn. His field research career is legendary in circles of wildlife scientists and managers. Read this book and you'll understand why."

—**Rich Landers**, Outdoors writer and former Outdoors editor for *The Spokesman-Review*

"Wild animals do not give up their secrets easily and McCorquodale shows just how much work—and danger—is involved in our quest to conserve wild things and the landscapes they rely on. This is a collection of well-written and exciting stories to chronicle one man's efforts to chase down these secrets and make meaningful contributions that will benefit future generations."

—**Jim Heffelfinger**, Wildlife Science Coordinator, Arizona Game & Fish Department and Chair of the Western Association of Fish and Wildlife Agencies Mule Deer Working Group

"Early in my days as the Outdoor Columnist for the *Yakima Herald-Republic*, Scott McCorquodale invited me to spend a day with him as he checked on denned black bears on the Yakama Nation Reservation. It was incredibly exciting and educational. That day popped into my mind many times as I read Scott's new book *Chasing Wildlife Secrets*. The author shares dozens and dozens of stories about his many years in the field as a big game biologist, told with great admiration and respect for the animals he is studying, and the people with whom he worked. Even after spending time with Scott, never could I have imagined all the exciting, interesting, and sometimes harrowing experiences he has lived. *Chasing Wildlife Secrets* was a great read and one I recommend highly!"

—**Rob Phillips**, outdoor writer and author of the Luke McCain Mystery Series

"As a longtime local hook-and-bullet magazine editor, I thought I knew a lot about Washington wildlife research and what all goes into it, but in his new book, Scott McCorquodale really opened my eyes to the thrills and chills as well as the drudgery that the scientific monitoring of elk, deer, bears, and more entails. Mixing in laugh-out-loud moments with deep insights, Scott chronicles his 40-year career from grad student to regional wildlife manager, from studying Hanford's inexplicable wapiti herd to dealing with Buttons The Elk That Thought She Was A Human—a period of time that also saw the vast technological improvements he also traces. Indeed, it's not just a book about Scott darting, collaring, and tracking critters—of which he did plenty—but also the folks who trusted him to do the science or assisted him in the field—his tribal and state bosses, fellow "muggers," and especially the gifted and daring pilots like Jess Hagerman who helped make it all possible. While Scott has written plenty of scientific papers, here his words flow across the pages like elk running through Washington's woods and glades in highly readable prose that is also educational. Through Scott's book, I have a higher appreciation for those who make studying wildlife their career so that hunters can harvest a few, the public can enjoy viewing them, and the critters can continue to be critters."

—**Andy Walgamott**, editor of *Northwest Sportsman* magazine

A BIOLOGIST'S JOURNEY

SCOTT McCORQUODALE

Washington State University Press
Pullman, Washington

Washington State University Press
PO Box 645910
Pullman, Washington 99164-5910
Phone: 800-354-7360
Email: wsupress@wsu.edu
Website: wsupress.wsu.edu

First printing 2025

Library of Congress Cataloging-in-Publication Data is available.

The Washington State University Pullman campus is located on the homelands of the Niimíipuu (Nez Perce) Tribe and the Palus people. We acknowledge their presence here since time immemorial and recognize their continuing connection to the land, to the water, and to their ancestors. WSU Press is committed to publishing works that foster a deeper understanding of the Pacific Northwest and the contributions of its Native peoples.

Cover design by Patrick Brommer
Interior design by Tracy L. Randall

Dedication

To my wife Kim, who inspires me and taught me
to dream big and chase my dreams relentlessly.
Thank you for believing in me and loving
the wild things—creatures and places—with me.
This story is our shared journey.

Contents

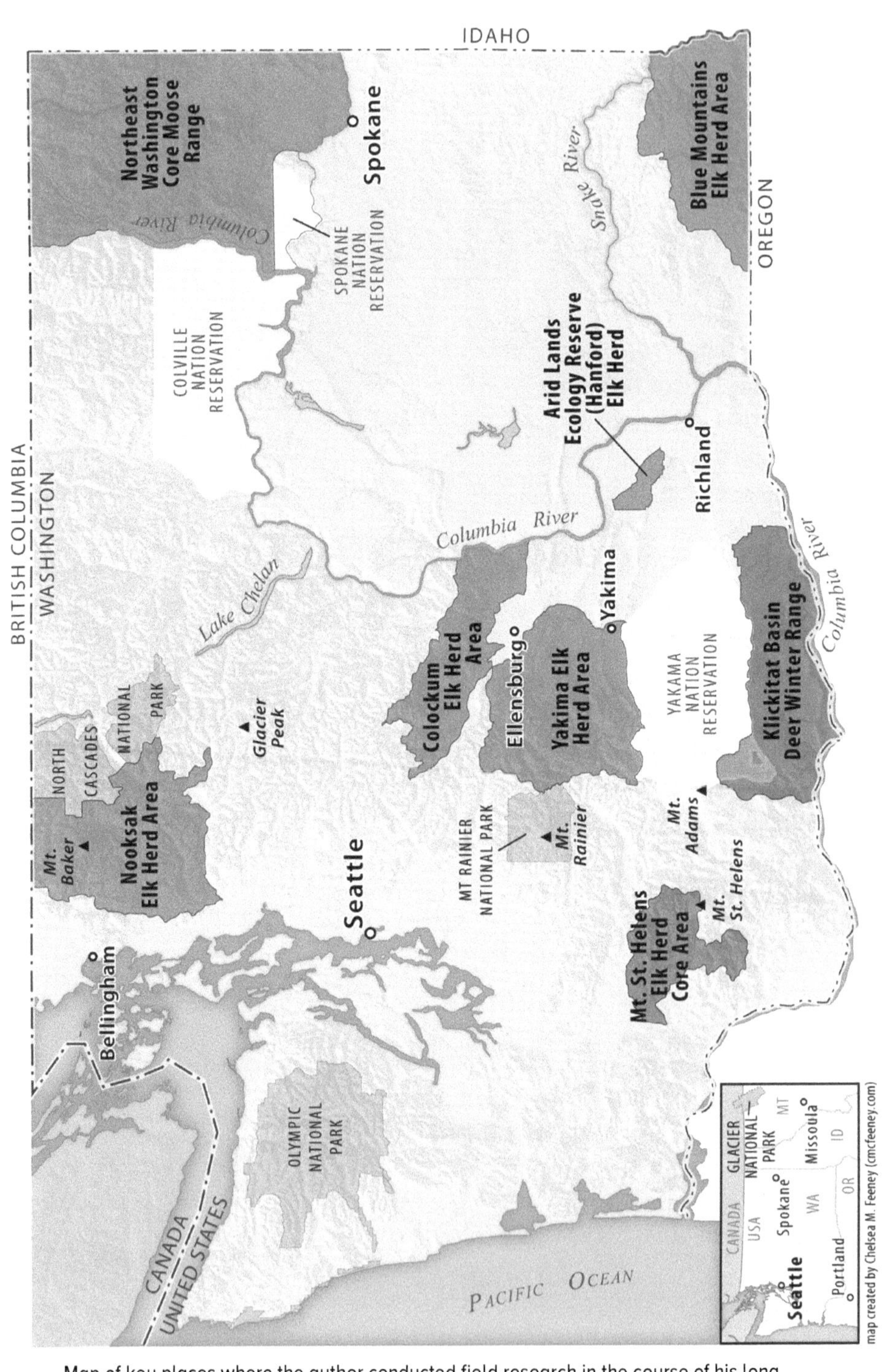

Map of key places where the author conducted field research in the course of his long career as a wildlife biologist.

Introduction

Heart pounding as I pushed my snowshoes up the last incline and into the snowy bowl, I stopped to take a much-needed deep breath and looked around the stunning winter landscape. A moment later, my research assistant, Dave Blodgett Jr., crested the hill twenty yards to my left. It was a perfect winter morning—cold but sunny. We had left our snowmobiles behind half an hour ago, after nearly an hour's ride on a road blanketed with three feet of untracked snow. Our pickup trucks, tires chained, were nearly a thousand feet below the snowmobiles, at the end of a barely drivable logging road buried under a foot of snow.

It had been a purposeful, albeit challenging journey; according to my handheld GPS unit, we were now within a couple hundred yards of our quarry—or so we thought. The firs and hemlocks cast bluish, mottled shadows over the snow-covered forest floor, and the clearings sparkled as innumerable fresh snowflakes reflected the brilliant morning light. The new snow softened the landscape—stumps and logs became gentle, rolling white humps, and standing trees stooped under the weight of the heavy snowfall. There were no tracks—other than ours—and no bird sounds. In the profound stillness, all I could hear was my own misty breathing—now slowing again. Although there was no outward evidence of another living thing here, Dave and I knew we were not alone.

I pulled the radio-tracking receiver from my pack and turned it on. Tuned to 149.780 megahertz, it made the sound I hoped to hear—a pulsating electronic "chirp, chirp, chirp...." We had been guided to where we now stood, knee-deep in snow, by a set of GPS coordinates I obtained a week earlier while tracking the same radio frequency from the cramped back seat of a Cessna 182 airplane. According to both the coordinates and the chirping of my receiver, she was close—somewhere in this remote, wintery bowl. We knew her by radio frequency but also by her nickname—Midnight. If she didn't already know we were here, she soon would.

Midnight was an adult female black bear—about eight years old. Our current task was to search for her exact location in this white, undulating landscape. We'd done this often enough to know that we were probably looking for a hollowed log, the root ball of a fallen tree, a stump with a hole beneath it, or perhaps a cleft in a rocky outcrop. The receiver would help us narrow the search. I used the handheld antenna to pinpoint the strongest signal as we trudged slowly through the deep snow. We passed a pair of likely looking snowy bumps—hulks of fallen logs—but neither proved to be Midnight's winter den.

As we crossed the bowl, Dave looked in my direction, waved, and pointed at what appeared to be a snow-covered downed tree, one with a shape that told us there were roots still attached to the tree's base, spreading upward and outward like octopus tentacles. The radio signal corresponded to where Dave was pointing. It grew louder as we covered the fifty yards to the snow-laden log. I looked at Dave and nodded as we drew close. At the tree, I walked along its length with the receiver volume turned so low I could barely hear it. It was faint in every direction except right near the root ball. This was it—she was here.

There was a tiny opening in the snow—just big enough for us to see into the hollow where the main roots spread out from the base of the tree. We removed our snowshoes as quietly as possible, but we knew she likely was already aware of our presence. I pulled out my flashlight and pointed its beam into the small gap in the snow. Just eight feet away, I saw Midnight's dark shape as she groggily lifted her head and squinted back at me. She didn't move or growl or hiss or show any aggression. She was calm, still, lethargic; but her eyes were open—she knew we were here. Near her belly, I could make out her companions—two tiny, wiggly black bear cubs who were clearly more awake than their mom. They were three or four weeks old, their eyes barely open. We were the first humans to see them.

Our mission did not require the recapture of Midnight to change her collar or handle her tiny cubs. I took a couple photos, scribbled a few notes, and tied a small piece of flagging on a nearby tree branch. We then put on our snowshoes, shouldered our packs, and began the snowy downhill trek toward our waiting snowmobiles. We would come back in the summer to explore the structure of the den and collect habitat data now concealed by the winter blanket of white. But today we'd bother Midnight and her family no more than this. We had accomplished our goal—to find this exact spot and mark it.

Midnight's instincts had led her to this place earlier in the fall. It was perfect—high enough to have a persistent snowpack through the winter months, sheltered enough to prevent any snowmelt from falling into her natal nest of fir boughs, and remote—away from roads and above a steep hillside. She intended that no other creature would know she was here—this was to be her secret place to spend the winter and give birth to her next litter. Dave and I had discovered it only because of the small radio collar around her neck, which we had placed the previous June when we trapped and sedated her in the valley below.

Midnight was part of the bear population we were studying. The information we gathered about these shy, wide-ranging, secretive carnivores—ages, movements, diets, range sizes, preferred habitats, survival and birth rates, and where and when the bears denned—was not easily discovered. Fortunately, we had research tools and techniques that helped us learn all these things—plus an abundance of patience and determination. We'd need all of it to chase—and learn—their secrets.

For as long as I can remember, I have been fascinated by animals, especially wild ones. I had an assortment of pets growing up: dogs, cats, miniature turtles, toads carried home from the local golf course in my pants pockets—to my mother's chagrin—and a parakeet. But I was particularly enamored with wild animals—birds, reptiles, amphibians, and mammals—especially mammals. It would be a circuitous path, but my passionate curiosity about wild animals eventually led to my adult career as a wildlife biologist.

Even before I sat in my first wildlife biology classroom, I knew that I wanted to be a field research biologist, studying animals in the natural world and learning new and interesting things about wildlife—I wanted a front row seat observing wild animals being wild. Back then, I could only imagine the amazing things I'd eventually observe during thirty-plus years of doing field research. To spend my career chasing wildlife secrets was my dream from the beginning. I had an inkling that it would take hard work to get there—and the help of some key people along the way, but I had no idea then how fascinating it would be.

Some wildlife secrets are perplexing puzzles that take decades and many different researchers to unravel: why can bears sleep in dens for five months without urinating or defecating and never accumulate toxic metabolic waste products; how do long-distance migrants, like many bird species, navigate thousands of miles each year, between their traditional wintering and nesting grounds in opposite hemispheres?

Such perplexing questions are challenging to answer solely with field studies. Usually, elaborate experiments are the only way to test among competing hypotheses, especially those involving physiologic, metabolic, or neurologic mechanisms. But many wildlife secrets can only be meaningfully pursued in the field under natural conditions. These often embody practical questions—how many animals are in a population; what are their birth and death rates; how large are their ranges; are they migratory or resident; what habitats are most important among those available; what do they forage on and how does that change with seasons; how fit are individuals; and what factors—if any—are limiting or regulating population growth and resilience? And, as in the story about Midnight and the other bears in her population, where were their winter dens and were suitable sites abundant or limited?

The answers to all these questions—and others—can have important conservation implications and are extremely relevant to managing wild populations and the habitats they depend on. This is demanding work. Wild animals don't give up their secrets easily. Discovering the answer to any one question can take years.

In physics and chemistry, a laboratory setting allows a researcher to control all the extraneous variation in a system, manipulating only the variable of interest and isolating an outcome. That makes for powerful tests of a hypothesis. A biologist studying wildlife under natural conditions can control almost nothing—the system is complex and dynamic. Nature is riddled with inherent variation, and that variation changes all the time. Weather, for example. Field rcsearch is the proverbial quest for a signal amidst the noise, and the noise is deafening. Wildlife populations also consist of individuals, and individuals are unique, introducing another source of variation that cloaks wildlife secrets.

My work was challenging but also incredibly fascinating. I pursued mostly large wild mammals through forests and vast shrub-steppe—including the rugged Klickitat Breaks—and the wildest places of pristine wilderness in the Cascade Mountains, the Selkirks, the Blue Mountains, and the rugged Nooksack River country. I was seeking answers to an array of questions—many on the list above. Along the way, I learned other incredible things about wildlife almost accidentally. Each time I went into the field I wasn't certain what I would see or experience, but often it was something new or unexpected, and it was always intriguing. I tried not to affect the behavior of the animals I was studying. My goal was to be a sublime presence on the landscape they occupied and cause minimal negative impact on their activities.

When you are studying the what, where, when, and why—the most difficult question—of wild animal behavior in the natural world, you can't just pick the days with nice weather or chase the study animals in easy-to-get-to places. I did field work in miserably hot and bone-chillingly frigid conditions, and I rarely did it alone. Usually, I led a small team that included wildlife technicians or local wildlife biologists, but there were still many days I headed out alone in pursuit of a study animal or went to the place where it had been the day before or where it had died. I traveled thousands of miles in research trucks, drove four-wheelers and snowmobiles, deployed from boats, rode horseback at least once, pedaled mountain bikes, and spent more than a thousand hours in small airplanes and helicopters. And I hiked—a lot. I went where the animals went.

Sometimes our research questions predated good tools for answering them. When we could, we developed new tools to fill our needs. We also benefited from tools others developed. Technology and field techniques became more sophisticated over time—our questions paced these advancements and became more complex as well. The data from each research effort accumulated steadily but slowly—like pieces of a puzzle, filling in knowledge gaps. Sometimes it changed what we—the scientific community—thought we understood well. I published many papers in peer-reviewed scientific journals, documenting what we learned—which wildlife secrets were not so secret anymore.

What drove me was an innate curiosity about wild animals. They captivate me—always have, still do, and probably always will. I have noticed that many people are interested in wildlife. When someone asked me what I did for a living and I replied that I was a wildlife researcher, they'd say something like, "Wow, that must be the coolest job ever." I've had more of those conversations than I can count. That question was usually followed by: what do wildlife biologists do, what was your research about, or tell me an interesting story about your field work. I didn't mind. They were right—I did have a cool job. And I loved talking with people about wildlife.

During my career, there were many days when I reveled in the experience and celebrated the accomplishments. There were also days of mourning. I lost too many professional peers and friends along the way. Wildlife field work has built-in risks. Flying, in particular, is hazardous duty; and anytime you head to remote places, there are real dangers. Working closely with wild animals, particularly while capturing them for research, warrants caution and recognition that these are large, untamed, unpredictable creatures—they do not understand our benevolent motivation as wildlife conservationists. They simply know that we are people—and people are scary.

I experienced incredible highs working as a wildlife biologist, as well as disappointments and sorrow. When I retired in 2022, I resolved to write a book about my amazing professional journey. This isn't a science or biology book. There are no graphs or tables of data—no descriptions of statistical analyses or hypothesis tests. The technical aspects of the work I did as a wildlife research biologist are captured in numerous scientific journal articles and academic book chapters. I'm proud of that body of work, but that is not what this book is about. This book is about the experience of a lifework in the field, studying amazing, captivating wild animals. It's a personal story.

I observed the natural world from a unique and intimate perspective and had incredible experiences along the way—almost daily, it seemed. My respect for wild animals and reverence of wild places only grew with time, as did my appreciation that I was part of something special. The experience awed and humbled me, and I'm deeply grateful for the opportunities that came my way while chasing wildlife secrets. In the following chapters, I will share what made this journey so extraordinary: the highs as well as the lows—and the days of discovery and wide-eyed wonder.

Chapter 1

Twenty-seven Elk

It was a typical late-July day in the arid shrub-steppe of eastern Washington. No clouds. Blazing sun. At three in the afternoon, the temperature was 105 degrees Fahrenheit. My day was just beginning because today I was working the night shift. Driving along the dirt track and listening to the telemetry receiver in the cab of my truck, I heard a familiar sound—the electronic "chirp, chirp, chirp...." of the signal from a radio collar on a cow elk somewhere on the mixed bunchgrass-sagebrush plain of Washington's Arid Lands Ecology Reserve. I stopped to get a better bearing on the signal. Grabbing my basic gear—a receiver, handheld antenna, and binoculars—I hiked toward a small, grassy knoll a few hundred yards away.

Shrub-steppe elk on the Arid Lands Ecology Reserve in October 1999. The author studied these elk for his 1980s master's thesis research project. | Scott McCorquodale photo.

From this high point—subtle as it was—I swung an arc with the antenna and concluded the elk was some distance to the east. That put her in country very familiar to both of us. Looking north a half mile, I could see the place where she would probably end up later tonight—Rattlesnake Springs. This was promising for tonight's goal—determine when this elk and the others with her were active and inactive until sometime around eight o'clock tomorrow morning. Besides the elk I was tracking, there were four others bearing radio collars in the group, and I could hear all five from my little hill.

Encouraged, I headed back to the truck to get organized and pick the right parking spot for the night. As I reached the road and approached my rig, I saw him—a decent sized northern Pacific rattlesnake coiled up in the late-afternoon shade cast by the truck—two feet from the driver's door. I'd only been away for twenty minutes, but that was long enough for the snake to slither out of the heat to seek the now-shady spot on the road. Like most rattlesnakes I encountered on the reserve, he was not looking for a fight. At my approach, his instincts motivated him to escape, and he slowly slithered back into the desert from whence he came.

Driving to a spot a quarter mile away—higher than the springs and providing a good view—I parked in the middle of the road—no chance of blocking traffic in this remote place. At half past four, I started recording data. At first, I sat in the shade of the truck with the doors open, but it was still hot. After sunset, I moved everything to the hood of the rig and spent most of the night sitting against the windshield in the dark—listening to the receiver and noting at twenty-minute intervals whether the collared elk were active.

When an elk was stationary—particularly bedded—the orientation of the collar relative to my position was unchanging and the audible signal notably monotonous. When the elk moved around—feeding, walking, trotting—the signal strength fluctuated up and down because the orientation of the animal's head—and likewise the antenna on the collar—was dynamic.

I had two other important pieces of gear—an early-generation night vision scope and a high-powered spotting scope. I used both to confirm each elk's location, based on my interpretation of the radio signals. The night vision scope was helpful for seeing in the dark, but those early scopes had unimpressive magnification. Before dark, the spotting scope, with its powerful zoom, was much easier to use. Throughout the afternoon and night, I kept recording the status of each collared elk, checked the direction of the signals, and tried to confirm locations with the scopes.

An interesting thing occurred on these night watches—and it happened every shift. At two- to three-hour intervals after dark, a short-eared owl glided silently overhead while I sat against the windshield. Probably curious about the unusual presence of the truck and its odd hood sitter. I never heard them—owls have specially adapted primary feathers to make them silent in flight. I only detected the inquisitive flyovers by the sudden dark shape coasting by—visible in the moonlight—three feet or so above my head. There was always a single pass per episode, with at least a couple hours in between. The owls were my only detectable companions on those quiet, warm nights.

Nighttime data collection became routine—not particularly exciting, but productive for understanding what the elk were doing through a full twenty-four-hour cycle. As dawn approached, I logged data that depicted a pattern of movement to Rattlesnake Springs by dark, all-night on-and-off foraging bouts, and—typical of elk—feeding again by sunrise. At dawn, I was at the spotting scope, watching each elk getting one final meal from the streamside vegetation and adjacent grassland. By half past six, with full bellies, they were a herd again, moving gracefully and synchronously away from the springs, back toward the wrinkled landscape of grass and sage. By seven o'clock, with heat waves already visible through my scope, they were all bedded in the shade of larger sagebrush, hundreds of meters—perhaps a half mile or more—from Rattlesnake Springs, invisible to the casual observer. Only the radio collars betrayed their presence.

These elk are the reason I live in Washington. I'd never been to the state before the spring of 1982. A soon-to-graduate senior in the Wildlife Biology program at the University of Montana (UM), I had been seeking a master's degree research project for several months at a handful of preferred universities. Having been invited to visit the University of Washington (UW) to chat with College of Forest Resources faculty about a possibility that spring, my wife Kim and I headed west from Missoula, bound for Seattle. It was her first trip to Washington too.

Dick Taber led the Wildlife Science Group at the college. I met him in Missoula once before, and we seemed to get along well. While my wife toured the campus, I met with Dick and a couple other faculty members. They had a funded project, and it was mine if I wanted it—a first-ever study of elk living year-round in a desert environment of eastern Washington. The population was small and of recent origin, and almost nothing was known about it. They'd arrived in the winter of 1972–73 from no one knew where. The expectation was that they'd be gone at the end of winter because the desert becomes a harsh place for elk to live in the summer. But they weren't gone. This small group of elk defied that first expectation and many others. I knew right away that this study was a terrific opportunity—my wife and I chatted for less than a half hour before I went back to Dick's office and told him, "I'm in."

During the 1970s, there was a dramatic upswing in elk research throughout the western states. Many studies were motivated by a desire to better understand how logging affected elk. Extensive roadbuilding and logging occurred at that time across several states. Much of the research focused on how reduced forest cover and increased road densities impacted elk. All the major contemporary treatises on elk surmised that they were susceptible to thermal stress—they were large animals capable of accumulating thermal loads that, without cover, would be difficult for them to dissipate. Due to their size and physiology, they were considered inherently at risk of hyperthermia. Although elk had done well in the distant past in the treeless Great Plains, the prevailing thinking in the 1970s was that elk had never inhabited any western desert ecosystem in large numbers. These regions were outside the thermoenergetic tolerance of elk, scientists theorized, and it was unlikely they could live here—certainly they could not thrive.

So, when a handful of colonizers walked onto the Hanford Site—a largely decommissioned nuclear production complex—and were still there a year, two years, five years, a decade later, they were doing something unexpected. The shrub-steppe of eastern Washington is a large shrub and arid grassland system just northwest of the Great Basin Desert. On average, summer temperatures exceed ninety degrees fifty-five days a year, and there are almost no trees. Elk should not be able to do what these elk were doing, according to the prevailing science of the day. No one understood their survival strategy. The UW research project would remedy that lack of understanding, and I would lead the field work—my first time in such a role.

Every scientist wants to pave new ground—study something no one else has studied before, answer questions no one has previously asked, collect data that do not yet exist. This was the opportunity I had been given; remarkably, it came right at the beginning of my career. I would define the research questions, design the study, collect and analyze the data, and write up the findings for other biologists to learn from. The elk study would be exciting and challenging—and a bit scary. But it was the kind of opportunity I had been preparing for. Fortunately, I had some smart people to help guide me.

The Arid Lands Ecology Reserve (later renamed the Fitzner-Eberhardt Arid Lands Ecology Reserve), known by the shorthand "ALE Reserve" or "ALE," is 120 square miles of nearly pristine native shrub-steppe—the largest such tract in eastern Washington. Created in 1967 from an undeveloped portion of the 586-square-mile Hanford Site, it is one of several National Environmental Research Parks in the United States. The Hanford Site was established by the federal government in 1943 as part of the Manhattan Project, a wartime effort to produce plutonium.

Although many industrialized portions of the Hanford Site became contaminated by the production of nuclear materials and their by-products, the ALE Reserve was maintained for decades as an undeveloped buffer to protect human communities south and west of Hanford. It was large enough to be a functioning sagebrush-steppe landscape, with virtually all its ecological components intact. Because of Hanford security, public access was restricted, making it a relatively disturbance-free zone for wildlife.

It was here, sometime during winter 1972–73, that a small group of elk wandered onto the landscape. They were first detected by local rancher Dick McWhorter, who owned a small airplane and contracted with the US Department of Energy (DOE) to fly weekly patrols along the ALE Reserve boundary. He documented the first elk sightings in his flight logs. These logs were the primary evidence that the handful of wayward elk were still on ALE the next year, and the next, and the next. The reserve was now their home. Almost no one had seen them besides Dick. Only a few people knew they were there, and even fewer knew just how significant their presence was.

April 1984 photo taken on the Arid Lands Ecology Reserve in the shrub-steppe of eastern Washington. These pioneering animals changed scientific thinking about the environmental tolerance of elk. | Scott McCorquodale photo.

"Melvin," photographed while running through Washington's shrub-steppe in February 1984, during the author's early 1980s elk field research project. | Scott McCorquodale photo.

The larger scientific world first heard of these elk in a brief two-page note published in the prestigious journal *Science* in 1977. The piece was authored by a plant ecologist who had worked on the ALE Reserve for decades—Bill Rickard. He was the catalyst for the graduate project I was about to undertake. Bill and I first met in fall 1982—my initial visit to Hanford. He became a mentor, confidant, advocate, and good friend. He also joined my UW thesis committee.

There were fundamental questions to answer about these elk. How many were there in 1982? What was the extent of their range? How successful were they—were they prospering or struggling? How did they manage thermal stress? What did they eat across the seasons?

I received my federal security clearance in October 1983—it was time to start exploring the ALE Reserve and look for elk. There had been many earlier ecosystem studies on the reserve, but none were ongoing when my work began. For the next three years, I would see almost no one while pursuing elk around this arid landscape as I tried to unravel their mysteries. The only human activity I saw was the once-a-month retrieval of weather station data by a meteorologist. It was just me, 120 square miles of shrub-steppe, and an incredible array of desert birds, reptiles, mammals, and invertebrates. For a budding field biologist, this was heaven.

Initially, I split my time between the UW campus, where I refined my study proposal and design, and ALE, where I familiarized myself with the minimal network of dirt roads and learned the landscape. I had made two multiday trips to ALE by late fall, explored most corners of the reserve and all the places I imagined elk would find attractive. I had not yet spotted an elk. The closest I came was seeing days-old elk tracks on the dirt road near Rattlesnake Springs and a few desiccated fecal pellets. In late November, after a couple days of fruitless searching on the third of these trips, I packed up my car and headed back to Seattle.

Washington Route 240, which formed the northern boundary of the ALE Reserve, was part of my route home. There were several small turnouts along the two-lane roadway, and I'd usually stop at each one and glass the sage and grass of the reserve with my binoculars on each trip home. This November day was cool—it had rained during my visit. The morning was misty, and whirling wisps of fog covered the landscape here and there, giving it a surreal—almost ethereal—appearance. I stopped at one of my usual vantage points and scanned the rolling steppe with my binoculars. The misty landscape had its own unique beauty this day, almost like a watercolor painting.

Then, right on the edge of a bit of fog, I saw it—a dark shape, moving slowly. Yes, it had a head and legs—my heart rate accelerated as the shape became recognizable. It was an elk. And it was not alone. I watched as another stepped out of the fog—then another and another. A few moments later, it was clear that all the elk in the group had emerged into view. There were twenty-three, one of which was a large bull with impressive antlers. I was ecstatic at my first sighting of the desert elk on the ALE Reserve. I'd been preparing for over two months, but my study began in earnest that day, and I had just become one of the very few people to see these elk.

There were challenges ahead, and in the months leading up to that first sighting, I had discussed them with my thesis committee and staff biologists working for Battelle at Hanford—in the 1980s, Battelle was DOE's principal environmental contractor. The primary challenge was to find a way to locate the ALE elk regularly. It was a large landscape, there were few roads, and we suspected the elk were very mobile. The answers we sought would remain elusive if I could not find them often—daily was preferable. There was an obvious solution—a strategy common to large mammal studies from the 1960s on—tracking collars. We would not need many, given the small population, but we would need to capture the animals to collar them—its own challenge. But it could be done. In October, we placed an order for four radio-tracking collars. We would have them by Christmas. Winter was the best time to capture the elk—they'd be in groups, and the females, if pregnant, would be in early gestation.

We planned for a mid-January capture. Helicopter darting was clearly the best option. The day before we were to try capturing our first elk, I spent two hours in a Cessna 172 airplane flying imaginary lines—transects really—across the ALE Reserve. We carefully covered the area where I'd seen the elk in November. They were not there; nor were they anywhere for miles in every direction. Our search began on the east end of the reserve. An hour and a half into the flight, we were only a couple miles from the western boundary, having seen no elk though we'd covered over three-quarters of ALE. Ahead, we saw extensive sagebrush in an area with a series of deep, parallel gullies. Just beyond lay the boundary fence. We were nearly out of ground to search. We flew down the nearest gully, then the next. Nothing. As we turned and lined up on the third gully, we saw them stand up from their daybeds in the sagebrush—nineteen elk—adult cows and juveniles. We veered away quickly to avoid disturbing them further. Those were the only elk we saw that day. We would start at the gullies tomorrow. I could hardly wait.

The next morning, a cold January day, I slid into the right side of a two-seat piston engine helicopter just after dawn, dart gun in hand. People would recognize the Bell 47G, with its Plexiglas bubble, as the helicopter from the movie and television series *M*A*S*H*. The pilot, Mel Hood, from Basin City, Washington, was a skilled crop duster, but he had never flown an animal darting operation.

There was no intercom in the vintage helicopter, so we had to shout at each other over the din of the engine. Neither of us wore helmets; I had no safety harness or tether; and unlike the fire-resistant, military-style Nomex flight suits I later used routinely, everything I wore that first day with Mel would easily burn or melt if exposed to flame or high heat. My confidence was buoyed by the youthful illusion of invincibility typical of a twenty-something male. We were both rookies in this endeavor, and we were making it up as we went. We didn't know what we didn't know—but we would learn.

Mel and I were airborne by seven that morning. Doors off, it was chilly. I rested the dart gun across my lap, fidgety and anxious, but also optimistic. All the elk we knew where to find were in a single group. We needed to be efficient to minimize chasing them—minimize their stress. I was proficient with a dart gun, but before today I had never used one from a flying helicopter to shoot at a running elk. As we flew the length of the reserve to where we saw elk the previous day, a truck with the rest of our crew was already heading down Route 240 to help process any elk we darted. They would get as close as possible by truck, then walk in. In the vehicle were Ken Raedeke—one of my UW professors—Battelle biologist Les Eberhardt, and Battelle veterinarian Bob Busch.

The flight to the sagebrush gullies seemed long but was only a few minutes. Mel appeared confident—focused. What you'd expect from a veteran pilot. As we crossed the dirt road to Rattlesnake Springs, I knew we were almost there. Over the noise of the turbocharged piston engine, I shouted to Mel, "There!" and pointed to the rolling sagebrush just ahead. As we dropped slightly and slowed, I nervously adjusted my grip on the dart gun. My heart pounded in anticipation. I knew we'd be in the middle of it any moment, and I didn't know what "it" would be like. We passed the first gully, and as we turned toward the next, I saw an elk, then two, then several. They were a couple hundred yards from where I'd seen them the day before.

This was new to Mel, but you wouldn't know it. As the elk—now nervous—began to move, Mel skillfully swooped around and aligned us to come up from their rear—dropping to ten feet above the shrubs. As they moved down a gentle slope into the gully, the sage thinned. We were just thirty yards behind them and closing. At that moment I noticed a large cow elk loping along near the left rear edge of the group. I pointed and shouted, "Her!" then pulled the gun to my shoulder and looked through the low power scope. As Mel maneuvered, the elk's hindquarters appeared in the scope. In the next couple seconds, as we got closer, I now saw nothing but half of her thigh and half of her beige rump patch. Putting the crosshairs along the rump patch line, I squeezed the trigger. Bullseye! The dart hit her right where I intended. The rookies did well.

As we had discussed before liftoff that morning, Mel immediately gained altitude so our darted elk could calm down and stop running, which she did. We flew big, lazy circles above her as she walked along in the sage, now alone. A half mile away, the ground crew knew by our altitude and circling that we had darted an elk. Over the next several minutes, the drug—etorphine (M99)—would calm the elk, slow her down, dull her reactions and perceptions, and finally put her on the ground sedated. Our truck-bound crew crept along the dirt roads, slowly closing the distance to the hovering helicopter. About ten minutes after the shot, she stopped moving. Her head drooping, she stood wobbly in the sage—no longer aware of what was happening. I directed Mel to land near where the crew vehicle had stopped, about a hundred yards from our elk. They could see her now, too. Once on the ground with the crew, we crept slowly toward her. We saw her hind end drop, then her front legs collapse; finally, she rolled onto her side. We had captured our first study elk, and I was over the moon—we all were.

Over the next several minutes, we monitored her vitals and processed the cow elk: after blindfolding her, we attached one of our four radio collars around her neck, installed small, numbered ear tags, injected her with prophylactic antibiotics, and pulled a small canine tooth—a tooth that most deer species don't even have—not used in foraging but extremely useful for aging. We'd send the tooth to a lab in Montana to make a microscopic section and count cementum annuli rings—one for each year since it erupted in the elk's mouth. Based on her extensive tooth wear, we could tell she was probably over ten years old. Weeks later, the lab's age result came back—she was between her thirteenth and fourteenth birthdays. That made her older than the number of years elk had been on ALE. She was not born here—she had walked here. What an amazing stroke of luck—our first collared elk was one of the original handful of colonizers. She was in excellent shape despite her age. We called her "Granny." She'd teach us a lot about desert elk, and she and I would see each other often for the next several years.

Five or six minutes after we injected the reversal, she lifted her head, climbed clumsily to her feet, and giving us a confused look, trotted off into the sage. Little did she know that we could now find her anytime we wanted. Everything had changed for my study. A couple hours later, we stood over another sedated elk—this time a yearling bull we called "Spike." We suspended the operation after Spike, agreeing that we had caused the elk enough stress for one day.

Three weeks later we returned, using Granny's collar to find the elk. She had rejoined the group quickly after recovering from the sedative. That morning, I quickly darted another adult cow with Mel—an extremely large and unusually blonde elk—our third study animal. Then Ken Raedeke jumped in with Mel and darted another adult cow—our fourth and final collar. We had carried out our plan, conceived nearly three months earlier. It had gone exceedingly well—four elk darted, all alive and well and transmitting their location twenty-four seven.

The group's work was finished. Now it would mostly be me and my arsenal of research gear: scopes, binocs, notepads and pens, a compass, fecal collection bags and rubber gloves, maps, and a camera—always a camera.

From early April through September, I was out on ALE nearly every day—tracking radio signals, pursuing elk. The routine was to drive the dirt access roads, listening for radio signals with a whip antenna on the roof of my truck. When I detected a signal, I used a directional antenna to obtain a compass bearing. When I was confident I had driven as close as I could to the source—a collared elk—I parked, grabbed my rucksack full of gear, and started hiking toward the signal. Sometimes it would be a modest hike, sometimes a long one. I did it in all kinds of weather.

My goal was to find the animal, get a visual, count and classify all the elk with it, pinpoint the location for mapping, take photos when I could—all of this without bugging them. If I bugged them, they'd flee, and this might affect the natural behavior I was trying to study. At the beginning, I bugged them a few times, but I quickly improved. I learned not to approach with the wind behind me, carrying my scent to them. Sight and sound were more forgiving. Eventually, I rarely disturbed them. I was deliberate and careful—moving slowly when I suspected they were near—always with the wind blowing from them toward me. Biologist stealth mode.

The author attaching a research radio collar after darting the dominant bull elk, "Brutus," from a helicopter on the Arid Lands Ecology Reserve in November 1984. | L. Eberhardt photo.

The collars made it all possible. But the elk were still mobile, and the ALE Reserve was big. They were not always near the place they had been the day before. I had another tool that helped—a lot. We had a Cessna 172 under contract, and when I lost track of an elk or several, I arranged to fly with tracking gear to find them. In this open country, I nearly always saw them from the plane. They tolerated the plane well—not seeming to know there were people in it.

The data came in slowly but continually. I learned new things constantly and grew familiar with the array of interesting wildlife in the treeless landscape—Swainson's and Ferruginous hawks, prairie falcons, goshawks, horned larks, shrikes, western meadowlarks, sagebrush and savannah sparrows, long-billed curlews, chukars, short-eared and long-eared owls, burrowing owls, common nighthawks, coyotes, badgers, rattlesnakes, bull snakes, mule deer, bobcats, even porcupines. I loved it. The elk I once searched for weeks to catch a glimpse of, I now saw daily.

Throughout spring 1983, I built tallies of elk from my observations—bulls, cows, juveniles— endeavoring to get a firm estimate of the current population. I relied on the collars but also made random observations as

"Melvin," one of the two largest bull elk in the Arid Lands Ecology Reserve—sporting a new radio collar—photographed in November 1985, with the base of Rattlesnake Mountain in the background. Melvin lived his entire life on the reserve and died of old age just before his eighteenth birthday. | Scott McCorquodale photo.

I roamed the reserve, mostly of adult bulls—none of whom had yet been collared. There were only a few. I learned that the big bull I'd first seen that foggy November morning was the dominant male. I called him Brutus and saw him often. I referred to the other large bull as Melvin. We eventually collared both bulls the next year. We learned that Melvin was a year older than Brutus. Both were impressive animals with huge antlers.

By the beginning of May, I was confident that I had my answer. There were twenty-seven elk—sixteen adult cows, five adult bulls, three yearling bulls, and three yearling cows. Twenty-seven was the consistent ceiling for the math on all the group counts. From a small band of colonizers in 1973, the herd had grown to twenty-seven in a decade. Soon there would be more—calving season was imminent.

The peak of elk calving is the first of June. But births in May occur, and some elk don't drop a calf until almost July. In May, I intensified my efforts to find all the collared cows every day. They would seek seclusion for calving—leaving the group for a period of solitary life. Newborn elk are vulnerable—being part of a large, easily detected group when you are an elk cow with a newborn is not good survival strategy.

One day just before mid-May, Granny was missing from her usual group. I searched for several hours before finding her farther east than the most commonly used parts of the reserve, in an area with almost no sagebrush—the result of past fires—characterized by large, rolling hummocks with deeply dissected ravines. As I hiked toward her, the slight breeze was favorable—blowing gently in my face.

After a half mile, the signal direction started changing rapidly—I was close and beginning to walk past her. She was in the ravine below me, and I stopped before getting upwind of her. She was in nearly the same place over the next three days. I still had not seen her. Her collar, like all of them, had a motion sensor that served as a mortality detector. If she were dead, I'd know it. She was just being secretive—following her instincts—guarding her secrets. I was sure this was her chosen calving spot.

On the fifth day, I drove down the dirt access road I'd been using to check on her. Listening to the receiver while I drove, I heard only static where I'd detected her signal for several days prior. Creeping along in my truck, I soon saw a set of fresh tracks ahead in the flour-like dirt of the road. Walking over to investigate, I smiled at the familiar large, cloven hoofprints of a single adult elk and—paralleling these tracks—another set about the size of a half dollar. Granny was on the move, and she was no longer alone.

Following the tracks down the road, I saw where the smaller tracks veered off to the left. Leaving the road, I walked slowly in that direction. Twenty-five yards farther, I found a tiny elk calf, a day or two old. bedded among clumps of bunchgrass. He was alert and curled into a ball, his head down in a hiding posture. I snapped a photo from a few feet away and returned to my truck. I knew that Granny was feeding somewhere nearby, and I could hear her signal—she had stashed her newborn so that if a coyote spotted her, it would not know where to find her baby. She would be back soon.

In the following days, I pinpointed the calving locations of the two other collared cows and saw them with newborns soon after. I was lucky to glimpse an uncollared cow with a tiny baby—likely near her birthing spot. In early June, there were no larger groups of elk. Other than the collared elk, I lost track of most of them for a few days. Each pregnant cow sought her own seclusion. Within a week or so of calving, they started regrouping. Once they could move well, the calves were at lower risk in a larger herd—more adult eyes to see predators like coyotes before they got close enough to snatch a young calf.

The most fundamental question I now faced was, how successful were these elk in an environment that was supposed to be too harsh? What biologists termed "success" or "fitness" was defined by reproductive success—driven by individual growth, nutrition and physical condition, and survival. Elk cows produce one calf a year at best—they almost never twin. Raising a calf is an energy drain, mostly the effect of lactation. Under good conditions, they can raise a calf to weaning and recover enough to breed again the next fall. Under poor conditions, raising a calf to weaning may reduce their chances of breeding that fall—they may skip a year or years. Biologists call this a reproductive pause.

In the 1980s, there were no robust ways to measure physical condition of wild elk in the field. Now there are effective ways to measure body fat using techniques like ultrasonography—but not back then. The elk we captured that first winter and each of the next few winters appeared to be healthy, with decent midwinter fat levels, and they were on the large side for elk. There was certainly no evidence that these animals were barely eking out an existence in an inhospitable environment.

I would have missed any calf losses the first few days—specifically to uncollared elk. But the collared cows rejoined the herd with all their calves in tow. Attrition over the summer is common in elk populations—forty to sixty percent is typical—most of it coming early. Predation, accidents, and malnutrition are common causes of calf deaths. That first summer, I saw all thirteen calves in a single day in early July when all the cows were together. More amazing still, I saw all thirteen calves again in late fall on another day when all the cows were in a distinct group—no calves had died. I'd never heard of that in an elk population.

Over the next four years—two were my master's project years and two were follow-up years—I documented the same pattern each year. I never recorded a calf death. Not one. That was unprecedented. In most elk herds, there are forty to fifty calves per one hundred cows by fall. There may only be thirty per hundred by the end of the calves' first winter. From 1983 through 1986 on ALE, the ratio I observed was seventy-six calves per one hundred cows by fall and the same by the end of winter. If I excluded potential two-year-old mothers—who would have bred as yearlings, with lower pregnancy rates—the ratio was an astonishing ninety-one calves per one hundred cows. Almost every adult cow produced a calf each year, and none of the calves died.

Over the same four years, the reproduction pattern, coupled with almost perfect adult survival, yielded a growth rate of thirty percent for the population. That was the second highest ever recorded for an elk population and it's near the maximum possible for an animal that only produces one offspring per pregnancy. It became increasingly clear that these animals were doing exceptionally well. They were not merely surviving.

With all thirteen 1983 calves surviving, the population grew to forty in 1984. Fifteen calves—all again surviving—brought the number to fifty-five by spring 1985. In spring 1986, there were seventy-one elk on the ALE Reserve. As growth occurred, we continued to collar more elk to ensure that we did not miss anything, even if multiple social groups became the norm—which appeared likely. With more collars, we stood a better chance of having an individual we could track in separate groups.

Calf production and survival were the right metrics for assessing fitness in females, but reproductive fitness for males is different. Elk are polygamous—dominant bulls defend harems of potential mates during the annual rut. Cows can—at best—produce a single offspring per year.

A successful bull can sire multiple offspring annually. But males compete for the right to breed and usually are only successful in their prime. Their breeding life is always shorter than that of cows.

Studies have shown that antler size is one of the best predictors of male fighting success during the breeding season. This gave me an idea. What if we could quantify antler growth in the bulls on ALE and compare it to that of similarly aged bulls elsewhere? Antlers are not necessary for survival, but they affect reproductive success. If they can, bulls should invest energy and nutrients into antler growth, but not at the expense of resources needed for growth and maintaining condition adequate for survival.

What made this comparison feasible in my mind was that in 1982 there were not many bulls. Within two years, we knew the ages of the full initial cohort either because we captured them—Spike the first year; Brutus and Melvin the second year; and Oscar, Linus, Clyde, and George later—or we knew when they became two years old and first grew branched antlers. Early on, we measured antlers of bulls during captures. Since elk shed their antlers every spring and grow new ones over the summer, we also started collecting shed antlers, which we could usually assign to an individual with a known age—again because we only had a few bulls at our starting point. We collected these data year after year. We even developed a mathematical model to predict antler weight from linear measurements. That way, we could estimate antler weight of live bulls when their antlers were still attached and couldn't be weighed—such as during midwinter captures.

Our dataset grew. We just needed data from elsewhere for comparison. I found two excellent options that were of the same elk subspecies as the elk on ALE. One was from the Canadian national parks, and one was from Yellowstone. Both had exactly what I needed—bull age data plus antler size and weight data. The result was nearly as incredible as the cow reproduction result. The bulls on ALE ran a full two years ahead of bulls from the other datasets. A three-year-old bull on ALE grew antlers comparable in size to that of five-year-old bulls elsewhere. The pattern held across ages of bulls. The ALE bulls grew fast and were unusually large at maturity.

A clear pattern emerged from all these data. These were exceptional elk—productive, fast-growing, well-surviving individuals—not exactly what we expected to find and certainly not what others expected us to find. This was not an environment on the edge of what elk could tolerate. The ALE Reserve was not merely marginal elk habitat—it was excellent elk habitat. I was unaware of any other elk population as fit as this one. They were exploiting the reserve's resources extremely well. It was extraordinary.

How did they do it? That was the obvious remaining question. Data from several aspects of the study—when integrated—helped us understand. There were both behavioral and physiological mechanisms involved. First, the activity pattern data—both from day and night sampling—showed that these elk were more nocturnal than most, especially in summer. They were active at dawn and dusk—as are elk everywhere—but these elk spent much of the night moving, foraging, and drinking during daily trips to the springs. There were two important springs—Rattlesnake and Snively. They were about two miles apart—one on the sagebrush plains and one in the Rattlesnake Mountain foothills.

We also found these elk to be remarkably good at finding shade beneath larger sagebrush. Some older stands had shrubs nearly six feet tall. The absence of trees did not mean the absence of shade. The elk also sought shade when it was easiest to find—early and late in the day. Bedding soon after sunrise, they found shrubs casting long shadows. They could not avoid the midday scarcity of shade, and it would eventually begin to increase their thermal load. But bedding early in the available shade allowed them to start the midday thermal onslaught from a lower body temperature.

It was clear that water availability was critical to their strategy. Unknown to me at the time, Kathy Parker, a bioenergetics professor at Washington State University in Pullman, was doing her own research while I chased elk around the ALE Reserve. Her work became highly relevant to ours. She used tame elk and mule deer to experimentally study thermoenergetics in elk and deer. Her work showed that deer shed heat loads principally via evaporative cooling through their mouths—panting, like a dog. Unexpectedly, she found that elk have a well-developed cutaneous network of sweat glands. They not only pant but can lower their temperature by prolific sweating across much of their body. That finding confirmed what we suspected—that nightly water drinking by

ALE elk was critical to their ability to avoid pathologic hyperthermia. If elk had access to water, they could maintain approximate thermoneutrality in the face of substantial heat loading.

As I began developing a working hypothesis about how these elk coped so well in a seemingly inhospitable place, I had several interesting conversations with Dick Taber, my graduate advisor. One day, he pondered whether the original premise that elk had never been successful in western deserts was based on flawed—or at least incomplete—data. He asked me if I thought it might be worth exploring the archeological literature? Maybe people who wrote elk books hadn't looked far enough back. So, in my time on the UW campus, I started visiting its many academic libraries. Archaeology was not a body of published science I knew much about—most biologists don't. But I was going to dive into it.

At first it was slow going and I found only scattered reports. Many sources were unpublished theses or project reports, and much of the work was associated with development of the hydropower system on the Columbia River. But I made progress. That progress picked up speed as one source pointed to another, and that one to another. The data largely came from midden sites where early Indigenous people had camped or lived—their piles of trash and discarded tools. There were extensive quantities of vertebrate bones—many large enough to be identified as to source species.

Remarkably, one of the most common animals represented in these sites throughout the Columbia Basin was the modern elk. Archeologists did not believe people would carry some of these bones far—such as lower leg and foot bones. They were convinced these animals had been hunted locally. The dating of these sites also put them in climatic periods like the current climate. These were not elk that inhabited forests of long ago during cooler times. They inhabited an arid steppe, not much different from the present-day ALE Reserve.

I compiled this information and drafted a scientific paper challenging the premise that elk had never been in the Columbia Basin when climates were similar to the recent past. The paper was accepted and published. Archeologists read the paper and decided to explore this idea further. Knowing their literature well, they found even more sources. Lee Lyman, now professor emeritus of the Department of Anthropology at the University of Missouri, was one such scholar. He published several related papers, agreeing with my conclusions and expanding on them. Lee contacted me, and we had many fascinating conversations. In the end, it appeared that earlier conclusions about elk distribution in eastern Washington were based on such sources as the journals of Meriwether Lewis and William Clark—nineteenth-century explorers who only skirted the basin along the Columbia River—and historic records that reflected faunal distributions already altered by people. Looking further back, there had been elk—plenty of them—in the shrub-steppe.

All the various information pieces came together beautifully. When I started my work, there were twenty-seven elk on ALE. Those twenty-seven elk helped rewrite the book on environmental tolerances and plasticity of all elk. Recent treatises on elk cite our work extensively and no longer suggest that elk did not or could not live in desert regions like Washington's shrub-steppe. We published nine papers on this work in peer-reviewed scientific journals and produced symposium reports and three popular magazine articles. There was also my master's thesis. More scientific papers have been published about these elk than any other elk population in Washington. Twenty-seven elk changed what we believe about an entire species.

Twenty-seven elk were just the beginning. When I moved on to other work in 1988, there were just under a hundred elk, and the population continued to grow rapidly. Dispersing elk, most likely with their roots on the ALE Reserve, started appearing in other areas of the basin—Horse Heaven Hills, Wallula, the Bailie Youth Ranch north of Pasco, and parts of Franklin County near White Bluffs. Hunters took many elk over the years when they left the Hanford Site; elk eventually crossed Route 240 and spread to the rest of Hanford. A full aerial survey of the population in early spring 2024 estimated a core population of 2,497 elk. All from twenty-seven remarkable elk pioneers.

Chapter 2

Beginnings

I'll just say it. My father was a *National Geographic* junkie. Perhaps that is where my wildlife journey started. I suppose we were part of the lower middle class when I was a child. I had one coat at any given time. My school clothes arrived once a year, delivered to a mail order Sears, Roebuck store a half hour drive from where we lived. I could mend holes in my own socks by the time I was ten. We never owned a new car, and we did without a lot of things—but never without Dad's *National Geographic*s. Not just the monthly periodical, but also the hardcover books they published from time to time. They were always around, and I spent hours looking at the photographs—eventually I could read the print. But the images were what drew me.

My favorite stories were about natural history or wild animals. I remember the first time I saw the work of John and Frank Craighead featured in *National Geographic.* I was spellbound by the account of the scientific work these twin brothers did in Yellowstone National Park in the early 1960s. They conducted the first-ever field study of wild grizzlies in North America. The photos of them trapping, drugging, and tagging these huge, dangerous carnivores mesmerized me.

My father, Bill, came from Canada. He'd been a Royal Canadian Air Force flight instructor during World War II, before immigrating to the United States. My mother, Betty, was raised in a small Colorado mining town, Delagua, that no longer exists. Her father was a miner whose first aid training made him the closest thing in town to a doctor. Her family eventually moved to California, where she met my dad. Both of my parents appreciated the natural world, my dad more so.

I grew up in a small town called Cathedral City in California's Mojave Desert. We moved there from the Southern California coastal town of Whittier in 1959, when I was two. I came to understand that we settled in the desert for one reason—it was dry there, and my sister Robin, who was more than ten years my senior, had health issues that doctors said would improve in a dry climate. We moved to a place where my family knew no one and lived in a trailer with nothing but a swamp cooler for air conditioning.

I was enchanted with wild animals from an early age. The regular doses of *National Geographic* stories and images must have fueled that interest. I still have many of those books. One in particular I nearly wore out—*Wild Animals of North America*, which the National Geographic Society published in 1960. It was full of species accounts and natural history facts and illustrated with the usual amazing photographs and the stunning artwork of painter Walter Weber. I discovered the book when I was about five and pored over its images many times before I could read. Once I mastered words, I tried to memorize the details about each animal—when did they breed, how many young did they produce per year, how big did they get, where did they live? I'd never heard of a wildlife biologist, but by age seven or eight, I knew I wanted to be a wild animal expert. That well-worn book is still on my shelf. It may be what spurred me to become a wildlife biologist.

I especially liked the large mammals. Living in the Mojave Desert, I rarely saw any, but when we occasionally drove into the mountains for the day, I might see a deer, and that was exciting. Mostly, I turned to books and periodicals and started spending my allowance on magazines like *Outdoor Life* and *Field & Stream*. These were full of stories and photos of large mammals. I also liked to draw, and my teachers said I had talent. Usually, I sketched large mammals and the occasional dinosaur and superhero. I loved any trip to the mountains—the closest were almost an hour's drive from home. I longed to live where there were pine trees, big animals, and snow in winter. I wanted to see the places and animals in Walter Weber's paintings. It took a while, but I got there eventually.

Although large wild mammals were rare where I lived, there were other animals—including desert reptiles. Those were interesting, too. I could walk two hundred yards from our trailer and be in an intact desert landscape. My friends and I spent hours roaming the desert near our homes. We became acquainted with several common lizards. The rarest were horned lizards—being kids, we called them "horny toads." More common were the dark, quick ones we called alligator lizards. They were nearly impossible to catch. The other common lizard was the one that intrigued us—the desert iguana. With their striped tails and mottled back and sides, iguanas are beautiful creatures. They were the largest of the common lizards around. Most importantly, iguanas were lizards we could catch, which we did—lots of them. They could be moderately fast, but unlike alligator lizards, they were not particularly spooky if you were careful.

We tried several approaches, but one was clearly the best and became our go-to technique. It was a two-man—okay, two-kid—operation. We wandered around, looking under the myriad desert shrubs—moving slowly so as not to scare any iguanas that might be lurking. When we found one, we went into action with our "pinning stick" strategy, which involved a small-diameter wooden dowel. The goal was to kneel and slowly move the stick toward and over the lizard. We had to move VERY slowly to avoid startling the iguana. It took patience and a steady hand. The target area was right above the pelvis, where the hind legs attached. If we were able to get the stick in position without spooking the iguana, a quick downward motion pinned it harmlessly against the ground. The second lizard "catcher" then moved in quickly to grab the lizard by the torso with one hand. If all went according to plan, we had ourselves an iguana.

I have no idea how many iguanas we caught. Safe to say, dozens. Often, we just studied our "catch" for a few minutes, then turned it loose again. The fun was in the catching. If it was large or otherwise unusual, we might take it home to show our parents or friends, then come back and release it. Hurting them was never our goal. None of us wanted that.

Our big, summer vacation iguana experiment came about when one of us—I don't recall who exactly—came up with a new and creative idea. What about a giant iguana terrarium? Hmmm. The plan came together quickly. We went into a local appliance store and came out with two cardboard refrigerator boxes. Cut one end and side off each box, put the cut ends together, and—voila—a ten-foot-long, four-sided terrarium frame. We filled it with sand, rocks, and shrub cuttings. With wilted lettuce and other leafy throwaways we arranged to pick up from the local grocer, we had our iguana food—we hoped—and we were set. We just needed some iguanas. That was easy. We were experienced lizard catchers by then.

We stocked our setup with several iguanas, and our experiment went live. I don't recall how long we kept and cared for our captives—maybe two weeks—maybe four. They readily ate the lettuce and other produce, and we checked them daily to make sure they were okay. They appeared to tolerate their captivity well, and we were proud of ourselves. As summer waned and the school year approached, we decided it was time to return the iguanas to the wild. We carefully gathered them up and released them back into the Mojave. I remember them scattering chaotically as they dashed off into the desert—an iguana stampede, of sorts. It was a cool experience for three ten-year-olds. Our iguana fascination probably kept us out of trouble. Those days fed my obsession with wild animals.

That obsession only grew stronger when my sister, now eighteen, married Richard Cromwell—a mountain man, cowboy, and smoke jumper—and moved to Montana. Richard was a son of a family we knew in Cathedral City. He had left the desert some time ago, but he struck up a relationship with my sister when he came to visit his parents. After the eventual courtship and wedding, my sister moved to Richard's home in Darby, Montana. A horseman, hunter, and fisherman, Richard knew a lot about wild animals and the backcountry. He wore a big cowboy hat and drove a big pickup truck. I was in awe. Unlike the desert, Darby, Montana, was large mammal country—big time. There were plenty of deer, elk, moose, black bears, bighorn sheep, mountain goats, and cougars in the hills and mountains around Darby. This new family connection was about to change my life.

After my sister's move to Montana, Darby became my family's one and only summer vacation destination. We spent two or more weeks of every year there. My anticipation of our annual trips to Montana was akin to what most kids feel on Christmas Eve. I hardly slept the night before we left. It was just under a two-day drive to Darby. Once we arrived, my dad and I fished every day, all day. My dad was not a hunter. He told me he went deer hunting once with friends, but it just wasn't for him. Fishing, though—he was a fishing nut. And Darby, in the Bitterroot Valley, sits along the Bitterroot River—a prime trout fishing stream. I hated leaving at the end of each visit. Our home was in California, but my heart now lived in western Montana.

The Montana trip was the highlight of my year. I loved fishing with my dad, but I also reveled in being in the mountains. I got to see many of the things that thrilled me—forests and meadows, jagged peaks, deer and elk, bald eagles, beavers, and grouse—wild places and wild animals I never saw at home. And there were incredible and unexpected experiences each trip. Every day we saw something amazing—like the day I went fishing with my dad at our favorite Bitterroot fishing hole and made a new friend.

As I stood, fishing pole in hand, I heard a slight noise behind me and looked to see a mink scrambling along the rocks until it disappeared into the streamside brush. Mink are water-loving members of the weasel family and usually live along rivers, creeks, ponds, and lakes. Fishing was a tad slow just then, so I decided to clean one of the fish we caught that morning and see if the mink might be enticed to come back to investigate, I knew mink ate such things. Placing the fish entrails on a rock, I watched and waited—but not for long. Sure enough, the mink reappeared and quickly absconded with the fish guts, even though I was only a few feet away. I tried again with another fish and got the same result. This captivated me.

Over the next week, we came back to fish this hole almost daily. I continued to offer the mink fish offal from our fishing success, and it always appeared within minutes to snatch its next meal. Luckily, my dad and I were decent fisherman. My daily engagement with this curious and resourceful mustelid delighted me. My dad just shook his head and laughed at my shenanigans with the mink.

During one of our Montana trips, I went camping for the first time. I rode my first horse on another visit. My sister knew a local fellow who owned a small helicopter; he offered my dad and me a ride one day. We flew over beautiful forests and meadows on the way to a high alpine lake near the tree line.

The ground below us was wilderness, so there were no landings. I spent the whole flight trying to spy deer or elk or a bear in the landscape below. This was my first helicopter flight, and I was ecstatic. I think my mom fretted the whole time we were airborne. Those times in Montana with my family are my best childhood memories. Our repeat visits continued for several years and reinforced my fascination with nature, wild places, and wild creatures. They also reinforced the feeling that where I lived wasn't really home.

In fall 1973, when I was fifteen, my father died unexpectedly at age fifty-three, leaving me and my mom traumatized and alone—both of my older siblings lived elsewhere with their own families. Over the following months, my mom and I pondered this new life—a household of just two people trying to cope with loss. My dad had owned a small business but not one my mom was prepared to take on. Increasingly, she felt we needed a change—like me, she did not love living in a trailer in the desert, and our surroundings now seemed foreign without my dad.

Mom sat me down one day and asked what I thought about moving to be near other family—Darby, Montana, for example, to be close to my sister? This was a courageous proposal for my mom—she was not a risk taker—but I knew she was struggling to cope in our current situation. I said I thought it was a great idea. But I was conflicted by the realization that I might now get to live somewhere I loved only because my father had died.

In summer 1974, Mom sold our trailer and my father's business, then we packed our belongings and started the familiar drive to Darby, this time towing a U-Haul trailer. There would be no return trip in two weeks' time. As the mile markers went by, both of us were silently navigating complex emotions. I thought about my dad and how this was my first trip to Montana without him.

We rented a small house in Darby, and I enrolled in a new school. I was to spend my senior year at Darby High School. The first year in a new school is often intimidating for a teenager, but it wasn't for me. The town was familiar after years of summer visits. My classmates were warm and welcoming—I'm sure some knew the circumstances that brought me there, and many probably knew my sister. I fit in better in Darby High than at the large high school I attended in California. I had a fun year—playing sports, making many new friends, fishing more than ever. I was even voted prom king. And I had a chance to reconnect with my sister after only seeing her a couple weeks a year for almost a decade. When she originally left for Montana with Richard, I was only six years old. I barely remembered her living with our family.

Life in Montana was incredible. I saw fall colors for the first time and experienced my first winter with snow, before which I'd only ever seen snowflakes fall once in my life. Also, for the first time, I was able to see wildlife everywhere—in all four seasons of the year. I discovered a place called Lick Creek, with a natural salt lick, just a short drive from Darby. My mom and I, and sometimes my sister, would go up there late in the afternoon and sit quietly under a tree. Just before dusk, elk and deer would wander in from seemingly all directions. We could hear the gentle mewing sounds of cow elk talking to their calves—a captivating sound as it wafted through the woods. I still missed my dad, but I felt that I was finally home.

A year—my first year living in Montana—passed quickly. As I neared graduation, I was unsure what was next for me. I didn't have a strong urge to attend college—maybe because I was ambivalent about what to study. My mom was still struggling—Montana hadn't healed her pain in the same way it eased mine. I gained strength and peace from the woods and the changing seasons, from fishing on the Bitterroot and watching the wildlife that intrigued me. This place was balm for my soul, but not for hers.

It seemed my mom needed something Montana could not provide. My brother, Bill Jr., urged her to come to San José, California, where he lived with his wife. In the end, she went, and so did I. Leaving Montana after only a year was sad for me, but I made a sacrifice that seemed needed. I wondered if I would ever live in Montana again—I hoped so.

I enrolled at San José State University in fall 1975 as an art major—intending to pursue wildlife illustrating. My mom recovered from her grief and loss. After a couple years, she reconnected with an old friend, now a widower. They began to date when he came for a visit, and they eventually married. I worried less about my mother now—she seemed happy again.

I continued to take art and general education classes at the university, but something was missing. I enjoyed sketching and doing wildlife pen-and-inks, but I didn't feel a passion toward it that would fuel a fulfilling career. While pondering my future, I met a wonderful young woman named Kim. We became good friends and soon fell in love. So much about life made more sense when I was around her. She was smart and kind and passionate about life, and she loved the outdoors—hiking, backpacking, skiing. I soon knew she was the love of my life, and we married in fall 1978. Though the way forward was uncertain, one thing was clear—Kim and I would figure it out together.

Art was an enjoyable hobby, but it didn't feel like the right career path for me. During our first year of marriage, I continued to contemplate career options. Kim was supportive and encouraged me to think about what I was most interested in—what would be a fulfilling job? If I could do anything, what would it be? We had each other and we were both willing to chase the dreams that would make us happy.

I found myself thinking again about those *National Geographics* of my childhood—particularly the stories about the Craighead brothers and their Yellowstone grizzly bear study. That brought me full circle, back to my childhood passion. I finally realized it was all about the animals—wildlife was my passion. After my father's death, the time I spent observing wildlife in the natural world helped heal my grief and trauma. Even in art, it was always about wildlife.

John Craighead had been a US Fish and Wildlife Service Cooperative Fish and Wildlife Research Unit leader during his years studying grizzlies in Yellowstone—at the University of Montana. Maybe this was it—what I had been searching for. It felt right. I knew the passion I'd need for success was in me. With Kim's blessing, I applied to the Wildlife Biology program at the university, in Missoula—an hour's drive from my old stomping grounds of Darby, Montana. I thought, maybe you can go home again.

When the letter from the University of Montana arrived many weeks later, I nervously opened it while Kim looked on. I read it quickly, then turned it so she could see—I had been accepted into the Wildlife Biology program, starting with the fall 1979 quarter. We grinned at each other. Neither of us knew what lay ahead, but the first step of the journey was clear—we were moving to Montana. I was returning—she was going for the first time. I'm sure we were both a little scared, but maybe for different reasons. That August, we loaded up a small U-Haul truck and packed Kim's Toyota Celica to the ceiling. Early the next morning, we drove away, headed for the Big Sky Country. I was on my way to becoming a wildlife biologist. I knew it would be hard work, but I couldn't begin to imagine the amazing things that lay in store.

The University of Montana had one of the best wildlife biology programs in the country when I arrived—it still does. I spent the next three years taking the core courses. The program was strongly interdisciplinary. Besides wildlife biology and wildlife management courses, I took another year of college math, a year of statistics, a year of chemistry, technical writing, plant ecology and physiology, quantitative ecology, mammalogy, ornithology, genetics, molecular biology, economics, and computer programming. Besides a sense of homecoming—being back in Montana—I felt I'd found my path.

I did everything in my power to succeed. My personal maturity grew with my knowledge and skills. In fall 1982, shortly before graduation, I was given the Wildlife Biology program's "Outstanding Senior" award. Well, maybe "given" is the wrong word. I worked hard to earn it—but I felt humbled to receive it.

Chapter 3

Klickitat Deer

My four-wheel-drive truck crept slowly forward—the wheels chained to keep us moving through the ten inches of new snow that fell the night before. The storm had passed, and the sun was out on this bright, clear morning, but it was cold—fifteen degrees Fahrenheit. I could see the other two rigs behind me in the mirror, also struggling to maintain forward momentum. There was a decent chance we'd get stuck at some point. That's when we would need the cable winches mounted on each truck's front bumper—we might even need the shovels we had in the beds of our pickups. This was a tough day to be driving these backroads, and it would be a long walk out if it came to that, but it was perfect for trapping deer.

As our vehicles churned through the dry, fluffy snow, we rounded the curve where I'd get the first look at the next trap on our trapline. Peering through the leafless oaks, I saw the familiar movement—a deer, an adult doe—bouncing around in the net-sided clover trap. Clover traps are pipe frame boxes barely big enough for a single adult deer, with heavy netting strapped onto the top, sides, back, and door. They are simple yet well-designed to capture deer for research. With an excited deer in the trap, I did my best to speed up a bit without getting the truck stuck.

Stopping forty feet from the trap, Dan Morrison and I jumped out of the pickup and waded quickly through the combination of old and new snow toward our momentarily imprisoned deer. We had this down by now. Dan and I got to the door at the same time. He reached down for the weighted bar attached at the bottom of the net-covered door and slid it up a few inches. The deer instinctively turned toward the back of the trap—away from us—and butted her head and shoulders against the netting, trying to escape. Our view from the trap door was of her rear end. Trapped deer always tried to find a way out opposite from where we stood. I went to one knee and swept a hand through the opening Dan had created. Grabbing one hind leg, I pulled it off the ground and then snagged the other with my second hand. I gently pulled the doe backward as Dan raised the trap door higher. When the struggling deer emerged from the trap, Dan grabbed her shoulders and gently rolled her over into the snow. He quickly pulled a blindfold from his pocket and slid it over her snout. Having done this together several hundred times by now, Dan and I were an efficient team. We didn't even verbalize a plan anymore—it was automatic. We each knew exactly what the other would do.

By now, the rest of our crew—two wildlife technicians—had joined us. The rest of the process was routine—ear tagging, attaching a radio collar, drawing blood from a jugular vein, administering an antibiotic injection, taking a girth measurement, and inspecting tooth wear to estimate age. We did not sedate these deer—there was no need. Two guys could easily restrain an adult deer while a third performed most processing tasks. One person who knew what they were doing could restrain a

A black-tailed deer inside a clover trap on a foggy winter morning in the Klickitat Wildlife Area awaits tagging by the author's deer research team in February 1990.
| Scott McCorquodale photo.

deer. Without using drugs, we could release each one fully alert as soon as we finished our handling tasks. It took fifteen minutes maximum—from grabbing two hind legs to watching the deer bound off through the snowy oaks. This deer was our seventh of the morning, and we weren't finished yet.

It was January 1993, and we were just above the Klickitat River canyon, about fifteen air miles northwest of Goldendale, Washington. We

A black-tailed deer, now bearing ear tags and a collar, is about to be released from a clover deer trap on the Klickitat River deer winter range in December 1989. The author and his team conducted field research on Klickitat deer for seven years, 1988 to 1994. | Scott McCorquodale photo.

were in the heart of the Klickitat deer herd's winter range, just south of the Yakama Nation Reservation. I was the lead researcher on the project —now a large mammal biologist for the Yakama Nation. The technicians were tribal members and, like me, employees of the Yakama Nation Wildlife Program. Dan was manager of the Klickitat Wildlife Area, a state-owned management property where much of our winter field work took place. He worked for the Washington Department of Fish and Wildlife (WDFW). Dan knew this area like the back of his hand, and I was familiar with it by now as well.

After I finished my master's degree research on elk of the Arid Lands Ecology Reserve at the Hanford Site, I went to work for Battelle's Pacific Northwest Laboratory (PNL; now Pacific Northwest National Laboratory, or PNNL)—a long name for Battelle's contractor presence on the Hanford Site where they were the Department of Energy's environmental lead. At that time—1986—I was still doing elk research, and mule deer research as well, at Hanford. There was considerable environmental funding at Hanford at the time. The Department of Energy had been tasked with finding a suitable location and developing a permanent, high-level radioactive waste disposal site—the first such site in the nation. There were two candidates: Yucca Mountain in Nevada and the Hanford Site.

Numerous Battelle scientists were working on this project—the Basalt Waste Isolation Project, or "BWIP" (pronounced B-whip), as we called it. There were millions of federal dollars funding the environmental work. At the time, the focus wasn't on evaluating the environmental effects of an operational waste site. Our work at Battelle involved monitoring the environmental effects of the massive engineering program focused on performing the assessment. That work included drilling tests, laying thousands of miles of seismic testing lines, digging test pits, and more.

I was a recent Battelle hire, so I lacked seniority. But the work was interesting, and the pay was the best I'd ever received. Kim and I now had a son nearly three years old. In late summer 1987, we found out Andy had a new brother coming next spring. Life seemed good. But in December 1987, word came that Congress had unexpectedly passed legislation that would dramatically affect the nuclear waste repository search. Instead of assessing two candidate sites simultaneously, only one site would be evaluated now, and a second site would be studied only if the first was deemed unsuitable. Yucca Mountain was to be the primary site. The Hanford work was going to be mothballed as quickly as possible.

In a matter of ninety days or so, literally millions of dollars would disappear from Hanford's budget—and Battelle's—including the funding that supported my current work. There was administrative chaos as most of Hanford's work units struggled to determine the full impact of the BWIP loss. No one told me I should worry, but I was a junior scientist. If things got tough for Battelle, my job would be at risk.

As Kim and I pondered what this meant for us, with a second child on the way, I received a surprise phone call that changed our journey. When the caller identified himself, the name was familiar but not the person. It was Bill Bradley. I knew of Bill because he earned a doctorate at the University of Washington under Dick Taber—the same professor I worked with for my master's elk project at Hanford. Bill passed through UW before my time—his research had been on elk in Mount Rainier National Park. He was now wildlife program manager for the Yakama Nation in Toppenish, about an hour from the Tri-Cities, where Kim and I lived. I'd never met Bill, but I knew of his Mount Rainier work.

Bill didn't waste much time, getting right to the point after a brief greeting. He was growing the tribal wildlife program in Toppenish. As part of that, he'd secured a US Department of the Interior Bureau of Indian Affairs (BIA) grant to fund a large, multiyear research project on deer in the Klickitat Basin. The basin included reservation lands and a large area to the south and west. He needed someone to take the reins of this new research effort and hoped that person would be me. He wanted to steal me from Battelle, and he wasn't hiding it.

After Bill provided more information on the project he had pitched successfully to the BIA, I said I'd have to think about it and talk it over with my wife. I called Kim right away—gave her the CliffsNotes version—and told her we'd need to talk a lot more when I got home. We liked the Tri-Cities, had made some good friends there, and I'd been able to expand on the elk work I started at ALE while working for Battelle. But the tribal project sounded interesting, and I'd oversee a large research effort again, digging into more unanswered questions about wildlife. That was appealing. There was also the considerable uncertainty about my future at Battelle.

A week later, Kim and I travelled to Toppenish to meet Bill and talk more. That visit went well—except that the office was a turquoise cinder-block building behind the local hardware store, with "Wildlife" spray-painted by hand on one side. But I was a field biologist—who cared what the office's exterior looked like. After debriefing with Kim and sleeping on it a couple more nights, we decided I would take the new job. I'd start in March 1988, but with a baby due in late April, I'd commute until he was born. Then we'd move somewhere near Yakima. As Yogi Berra famously said, "When you come to a fork in the road, take it."

I tried to hit the ground running. With a one-hour commute each way for almost two months, those were long days, but I was brimming with enthusiasm for this new opportunity. Leaving good friends and colleagues in the Tri-Cities was tough, for both me and Kim. I had been handed a fully funded research project—the fruits of someone else's labor. That doesn't happen often. The project had tons of potential, and Bill gave me a blank slate. "Make it your own—I'll support your decisions," he told me. I was excited but also a bit intimidated. This was a totally new landscape—not only a new work organization but also a new work culture—and I knew elk way better than deer at this point. To strengthen my resolve, I imagined my dad telling me, "You got this."

I settled into the new office around mid-March. It was too late for any winter deer captures, but there was still much to do. I had to build a deer research program from the ground up—and quickly. The Klickitat deer study would be my full-time job for several years. Bill did not expect anything else from me. My assignment was to create a study—and do it right. Our first year of funding dated back to October 1987, so we had a lot of unspent first-year funds in spring 1988. I used a chunk of it to familiarize myself with the geography by investing in some time in the air. I asked Steve Tolle, who I flew with at Hanford for several years, to bring his McDonnell-Douglas (MD) 500D helicopter to the Klickitat, and we surveyed the deer winter range extensively to get the proverbial lay of the land, maybe even spot a few late migrating deer. I also spent time in a Cessna 210, a fast, high wing airplane. Bill came along in the Cessna and shared his knowledge of the landscape and what they currently believed about Klickitat deer movements, little as it was.

During the first few months, my time was consumed by preparations for the coming winter. I researched and bought snowmobiles, built a good many deer traps, and purchased trapping supplies—radio collars, tags and numbered neckbands, blood tubes, syringes, blindfolds, and hobbles. I had to hire and train a technician, line out aircraft support, and get our trucks rigged for rugged terrain and winter backcountry driving. I worked with a metal fabricator to build clover trap frames to meticulous design specifications and bought a huge quantity of bulk netting from a Tennessee company that made commercial fishing nets. I spent entire days of entire weeks cutting and lashing netting to the clover trap frames and built more wooden box traps. I also ordered custom nets for helicopter drive-netting and two sixty-foot by sixty-foot drop nets. If we couldn't catch the deer needed come December, it would not be for lack of capture gear.

I also had to lay the groundwork for collaboration with the state wildlife agency. I already knew we'd want to work off-reservation on state land, but the Yakama Nation and the State of Washington had some history to overcome. This tension dated back to legal fights over treaty rights, mostly related to fishing but also including some hunting cases. The big federal court decision that affirmed treaty guarantees, despite state objections, was handed down in 1974—the Boldt Decision. Washington tribes and Washington's state government were still finding their way together almost fifteen years later. That was something I'd need to work on locally. The key relationship for me was the one I needed to form with Dan Morrison. Fortunately, neither of us had political or policy goals. We agreed the first time we met that we just wanted a first-rate deer study in the Klickitat. The other stuff was up to people with higher pay grades and their attorneys. Dan and I forged ahead with our collaboration and promised each other we'd focus on good research. We worked together almost daily every winter for about seven years. Along the way, we became close friends.

The deer in the Klickitat were, by all appearances, Columbian black-tailed deer. Just east of there, deer had the slightly different physical characteristics of Rocky Mountain mule deer. Classified as different subspecies of the same species, they were closely related, and their ranges were contiguous. That meant they probably interbred and shared genes along the boundary—a hybrid zone. Most likely, deer in the Klickitat were hybrids, but physically they most resembled black-tails—just a little larger than the classic coastal black-tails.

The Yakama word for deer was *yáamash*, and in the Pacific Northwest Chinook Jargon it was *mowich*—the derivation for Mowich Lake in Mount Rainier National Park. Deer are an important part of Yakama culture, stemming from the animal's longstanding significance in tribal diet and ceremony. Deer had been much more common in the Klickitat in the past. State hunting tallies and complaint levels from farmers suggested local deer numbers peaked in the 1960s. The same information implied the Klickitat deer population was at its low point around the time Bill Bradley sought funding for deer research. That was no coincidence.

Both the Yakamas and state deer managers presumed some generalities prior to our work. They believed these deer were strongly migratory, and they thought their key wintering areas were south of the Yakama Reservation—the Klickitat Breaks, the Simcoe Mountain foothills, and, farther east, Rock Creek. Deer summer range probably included the reservation and the higher Simcoes to the south. That's about it. Deer abundance was unknown, as were their survival rates, natality, range size, migration timing, and migration triggers. I was in charge of the effort to fill in the missing details. We'd be chasing deer secrets this time. To do that, we needed to follow quite a few deer and obtain samples from many

An adult black-tailed deer doe navigates a snow-covered meadow on winter range above the Klickitat Breaks in December 1990, during the author's long-term research project. | Scott McCorquodale photo.

more deer for things like pregnancy rates and health. And to accomplish that, we had to capture some Klickitat deer—as many as possible.

And catch deer we would. After the flurry of preparations during the previous summer, I was ready for our first full winter season in the field. Our primary tool would be the clover trap—and we had a bunch of them. We baited with alfalfa, salt, apple mash, and even anise oil, which was known to attract deer. Alfalfa worked best by far. The harbinger of success was snow. If we had snow on the ground, we caught deer—usually several—every trap night. Without snow, deer were harder to entice into the traps. We caught some deer, but they were likely to be ones we'd caught before—recaptures—deer who knew the trap provided a free meal and had learned that the scary upright creatures only touched them the first time.

Occasionally, we had to improvise on our normal approach—like the day one of the technicians slid the clover trap door open just a tad too much when we were getting ready to snag a trapped deer. I was a couple steps from the trap when I saw the doe spy the gap at the bottom of the door. Like lightning, her nose went down, and she dove for it in a bid for freedom. Her escape was short-lived. As she took her first full stride outside the trap, I took one quick step and lunged at her, hitting her behind the shoulder as I swung my left arm around her brisket at the base of her neck and my right arm around her right shoulder. She landed on her right side in the soft snow, with me across her torso. Everyone, including me, was astonished at my success. Any NFL safety would have been proud of the open field tackle I executed on that unconfined wild deer.

We trapped and handled deer every winter, all winter long. It was almost a hundred miles from my house to the trapping area—almost eighty miles from the Toppenish office to the Klickitat. My technicians and I made that drive almost every workday in the winter—no matter the weather or road conditions—for six winters. Occasionally, Dan set the traps on Mondays, a one-person job. He lived in an agency house on the study area. But my tribal team clocked a lot of miles to trap deer.

Clover traps were our primary approach, but we caught deer using virtually every known research method. We ground-darted deer; caught them in box traps; baited them under huge, suspended drop nets that we triggered to fall on them; used helicopters to drive them to nearby oaks, where we had propped up ten-foot-tall drive nets—three parallel nets, each four hundred to six hundred feet long. Three net lines meant we could catch at least three deer in the first net line. Other deer in the group would jump over the falling net the first deer brought down as they struggled, and we'd get three or so in the next net, and three or so in the last one. It took more people to run drop nets and do deer net drives, but we had lots of folks willing to help. It was exciting work. Handling live, awake, wild deer in nets while advancing important research was thrilling and rewarding. Volunteers were easy to come by when we needed them.

I vividly recall one memorable evening drop-netting deer. We baited with alfalfa under these giant nets propped up by four corner posts and a center post. I had a manual release line made of aircraft cable connected to all the suspension points. A firm tug on the line from our blind some 150 yards away caused the net to drop. Deer were wary of the net and would only go under it when it was almost dark. We'd watch them feeding around the net before dusk, and just as the daylight waned, they'd go under it for the alfalfa. One night we didn't see deer till it was almost dark. I could barely make out their shapes with my binoculars, much less tell how many there were. At dark, I was unsure whether any deer were under the net, but we'd driven a long way, so I just pulled the trigger and

A large black-tailed deer buck bearing a radio collar and ear tags awakens from sedation in a panel trap just prior to release by the author's research team in December 1993. | Scott McCorquodale photo.

dropped the net. Our crew that night was about six or seven people. We all flicked on our headlamps and scurried to the net. What I saw was completely unexpected.

Six adult bucks lay on the ground, tangled in the net—all still carrying antlers that had usually been cast by now. Our drop netting to date had yielded only adult does and fawns approaching their first birthday. They were easy to handle in the net and easy to get out of the net, even in the dark. Bucks were a different story—these were larger deer with formidable weapons on their heads. And the antlers meant a more complicated extraction from the net. They'd fight us as we tried to free them. Fortunately, I had learned to be prepared for any possibility—a good plan when doing field research with wild animals. We almost never sedated captured deer, but I always brought the drugs along—just in case. These bucks were getting drugged tonight because we only had about one person per scared and angry buck. It was safer for the bucks and safer for the deer catchers.

Helicopter drive-netting was the most exciting capture method. Our crew, often wearing camo, would hide quietly near the nets—behind trees, rocks, or logs. We eventually heard the helicopter coming toward us,

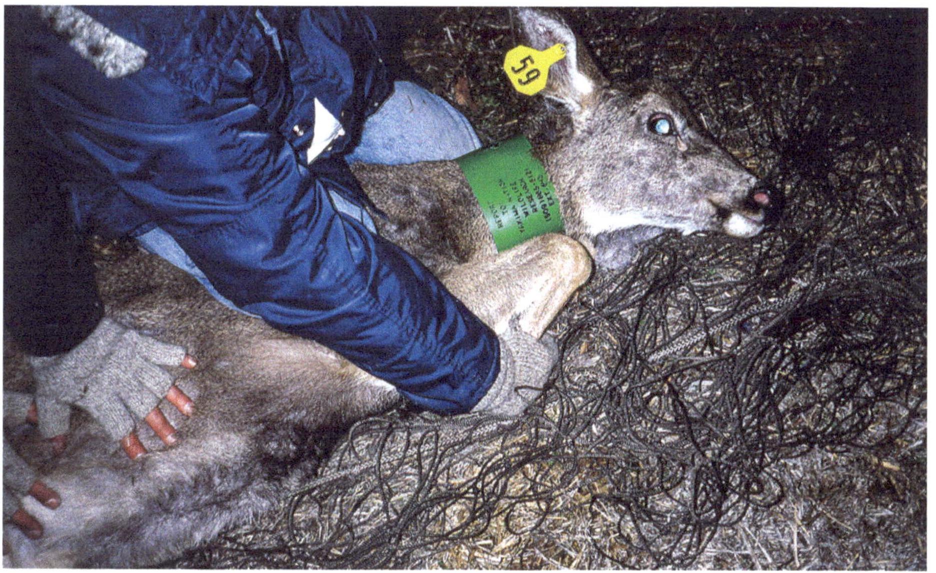

A black-tailed deer doe being handled beneath a drop net on a February night in 1991, during the author's multiyear Klickitat deer study. Drop nets were one of many methods the research team used to capture deer for radio-collaring and collecting biological samples. | Scott McCorquodale photo.

gradually growing louder, and knew there would be deer running just in front of it. The pilot would herd them gently, then push them hard just as they entered the oaks where the nets were set up. We would only see the deer in the last few seconds, running wildly through the trees toward the hidden nets. As the deer ran into the nets, they would pull them forward a few yards before getting tangled and balled up in them. As they hit the nets, we'd hear the roar of the aircraft passing just a few feet overhead. Each person then ran to the nearest netted deer and subdued it until enough help arrived to process each one. It was thrilling for us—a real adrenaline rush—and quite safe for the deer.

We became skilled at capturing deer. It was fun, exciting, and, at times, challenging. I even brought my five-year-old son Andy along once or twice while clover trapping. Over the winters we trapped them, we caught five hundred different deer. Counting the recaptures, we logged just under a thousand Klickitat deer captures. Most days we caught more than one deer. Our best clover trap days yielded about a dozen. A day of helicopter drive-netting might yield thirty.

Capturing the deer allowed us to put radio collars on some of them—essential for defining range size, movements, habitat selection, and survival. The most fine-scaled information came from this subgroup. But the larger capture sample gave us things like pregnancy rates—obtained from hormone assays performed on blood drawn from each female—and age structure.

The radio collars were simple VHF-pulsing collars typical of that era. We only knew where a deer was if we went out and tracked it to its location. I constructed several tall, paired-antenna arrays in our trapping area. Using these, we could triangulate where a collared deer was—approximately. Once the herd started migrating, it was mostly an air show. From spring through fall, I flew weekly in a small Citabria airplane—much like a Piper Super Cub. Each week we tracked as many collared deer as our fuel supply allowed. We also tried to avoid the Navy A-6 Intruders and EA-6B Prowler jets from the Whidbey Island Naval Air Station that regularly crossed low over the reservation. There were a few times when we got closer looks at them than we wanted. I imagine the naval aviators occasionally had similar thoughts about us.

Mortality signals always generated a hike to the deer to find out what had happened—if we could tell. Hunting—both state and tribal—killed the most deer. Winterkill, predation, collisions with vehicles, and one drowning took others. Does had about an eighty percent chance of surviving each year—bucks about fifty percent. We didn't fit young fawns with radios, but demographic modeling suggested first-year survival was a bit under fifty percent. Most years were similar, except for the one that included the winter of 1992–93, where this chapter began. That winter was severe for the region. At my home in Selah, there was a point where we had about three feet of snow in our yard. Most winters, eight inches would be a lot.

That winter, the Klickitat was buried in snow and the cold was brutal. Deer died—a lot of them. Adult does fared best, but more died than in average winters. The previous summer's fawns and adult bucks struggled to survive—fawns because it was more difficult for them to move in deep snow and they had less fat stored, and bucks because they had raided their fat stores during the late fall breeding season, the rut. Doe survival was just over seventy percent that winter. With few bucks wearing radio collars and no fawns collared, we could not estimate their survival, but it was dismally low. Deer were drawn to our alfalfa bait, and trapping was excellent. We occasionally caught a deer that was skinny, weak, and a candidate for winterkill. I didn't want to add the stress of human handling, so these deer we simply freed by opening the door. They got a free meal that night in the trap, but I knew that wouldn't be enough to change their fate. We found a multitude of deer carcasses that winter. We were observing a natural though brutal phenomenon, but as a biologist, I felt saddened to see these animals weaken and die. Coyotes, bald eagles, and other scavengers had plenty to eat.

Each deer used a small area in the winter and in the summer, but these areas could be far apart. The average distance between summer and winter ranges was seventeen miles, but we had deer that migrated over fifty miles each spring and fall. One doe we trapped in Rock Creek—about twenty miles farther east than the Klickitat—summered on the west side of Mount Adams. In the spring, most deer migrated in April—a few in late March, a few in early May—but they moved later after the hard winter. In fall, they headed to winter range from late September to late November, peaking in October. Fall migration did not seem to correlate with the coming of mountain snow—usually they were already on the move by the time that happened. In autumn, declining food quality on their summer range appeared to trigger these deer and seemed like a better explanation.

We suspected these deer were migratory. And most were. But there was no dominant route or pattern. Deer that wintered on the Klickitat and farther east on other winter range areas fanned out as they made their seasonal move to summer–fall ranges—in varying directions and distances. The plotted lines of deer moving from winter areas to summer areas and back crisscrossed like a spider web. The deer we tracked from the airplane in summer and early fall were all over the place—some on the Yakama Reservation and some elsewhere. A small number of deer didn't seem to get the whole migration thing. They just stayed all year in the same area we worked in during the winter—near where they had been trapped and collared.

We were also estimating population status and trends. A big part of doing that involved annual helicopter surveys of the deer on the Klickitat winter range. There had been almost no aerial surveys on the Klickitat prior to our project. We timed our flights to take place before migration but after the spring green-up that drew deer into the open. This was the best time to maximize our chances of seeing deer—we performed trial counts to demonstrate that.

We did repeated flights over the core area and flew only at the best times—early morning and evening. We used coverage protocols and mathematical tools to estimate deer numbers from the numbers of collars present and formal probabilities of seeing them. It wasn't just, go fly and add up the deer you see. It was a robust, scientific approach. As the years passed, our counts and estimates increased—the population appeared to be recovering. In the latter part of the study, we counted just under two thousand deer in a two-and-a-half-hour helicopter survey.

We were able to derive estimates of deer abundance that we expressed as winter deer density. These were the first formal, statistically defensible abundance estimates for Klickitat deer in history. Our estimates were in the range of forty-five deer per square kilometer on the Klickitat Breaks early in our work, rising to almost seventy deer per square kilometer by the end of the study. On the eastern edge of our study area, near Rock Creek, winter deer densities were lower—more like fifteen deer and just under forty deer per square kilometer in two units we worked on.

One of my most interesting aerial survey experiences occurred on a flight about halfway through our project. The northern limit of our survey area was a notable feature called Grayback Mountain, right on the Yakama Reservation boundary. The summit was a common starting point for our survey, and we'd usually see deer right away on Grayback, especially in a bowl below and west of the peak. On this late afternoon, we covered the summit portion and dropped into the bowl. It was typical to see several groups of deer here, but we were seeing none after several minutes. We swept back and forth across the unit, but still no deer. Steve Tolle and I were both puzzled. It was odd. Then, looking out my door, I saw a single animal moving across a rock slide a few hundred yards away. It was about the right color for a deer, but it moved differently. I pointed it out to Steve and told him we needed to get a closer look. As we dropped lower and swooped toward the mystery animal, I looked down while Steve banked and made a low, slow turn. It was a mountain lion—a huge one, undoubtedly a male—and it was carefully working its way through a maze of large rocks and boulders. "Very cool," Steve said over the intercom. Indeed, it was. We saw no deer in the bowl that day, and now we knew why.

State deer managers started implementing more conservative hunting seasons about the time our project began—a response to the evidence of population decline reaching a historic low point by the mid-1980s. For seven years, we studied Klickitat deer intensively—trapping, marking, following radio-collared deer, analyzing pregnancy and age data, and conducting aerial surveys.

The aerial surveys depicted a growing population, but were also sensitive to the one-year decline after a bad winter. Based on aerial survey data, the population grew at a rate of about nine percent a year. When we used demographic data—age-specific pregnancy and survival—along with a projection model I designed, the result was an almost identical rate of increase. That was encouraging.

We also fitted does we had captured but not radio-collared with colored vinyl neckbands that were easily visible from the air, and we changed neckband color each year. I was able to use specific color collars to estimate the pool of collars that were not that color (both were a known quantities)—a test of our ability to estimate total deer numbers from the number of all deer counted and collared deer counted from the helicopter. This density estimation approach validated our other findings.

The original BIA grant to study deer was for three years—that was all Bill Bradley could promise me when I took the Yakama Nation job.

Along the way, our progress allowed Bill to lobby the BIA to extend the grant. It was easy to demonstrate that we were doing good research, which benefitted both the Yakama Nation and state managers of the Klickitat deer herd. Many people played a role—technicians, other biologists from both collaborating agencies, administrative staff who handled the accounting and processed purchases of our research "toys," pilots, an equine veterinarian in Yakima who consulted and supplied all my veterinary needs, tribal council members who supported what we were doing, and people who removed obstacles when needed—Bill Bradley key among them.

I eventually published several peer-reviewed papers on the project in scientific journals. It was a remarkably successful effort, a growing time for me professionally, and it is still one of the longest field studies of deer ever conducted in Washington. Most importantly, it provided critical information for good management of the Klickitat deer. The population was more robust when we ended than when we began. A researcher can't ask for more than that. Oh, and it was fun—a ton of fun.

Chapter 4

Yakama Nation Years

The breeze rolling off the snowy flanks of 12,000-foot Mount Adams was numbing as the early November day dawned. The gray sky obscuring the mountain's summit yielded the first wind-driven snowflakes of winter while the flat morning light glimmered among the dormant aspens lining the Klickitat River below. Overhead, a bald eagle soared, scanning the Klickitat's shore for spawned-out salmon. Yet, the boy was oblivious to it all as he intently watched the old man brush back his long braids and kneel beside the fallen elk.

The boy's heart—alive with adrenaline—pounded with excitement. Yet, as he watched his grandfather begin the tedious task of field dressing and quartering the old cow elk, he was puzzled by the mixed emotions the old man's face betrayed. Their predawn trek from the valley below had been a success, yet there was no celebration—the old man went about his work with an almost remorseful solemnity.

After several minutes, aware of the boy's perplexed countenance, the old man began to speak. He talked of the coming winter, of their family's need for meat, and of a thousand years of elk hunts. He spoke of thankfulness to the Creator for providing the animal lying at their feet. He also spoke of the respect he had for the old elk and the humility he felt in taking her life for their family's welfare. As he looked into the young boy's eyes, he paused, momentarily reliving an elk hunt with his own grandfather many years past. He recollected how, on that day, his grandfather had shared similar words of wisdom, and then he smiled at the boy. Reassured, the boy smiled back as the old man knelt by the elk once again, unsheathed his knife, and returned to the task at hand.

Except for the four-wheel-drive pickup and the centerfire rifle, the scene is one that echoes through history—each generation teaching the next an ancient and uniquely Native American land ethic. For several thousand years, the Yakama people have hunted elk, deer, and other wild game in the forests and sagebrush prairies of what is now the state of Washington.

For me, the Klickitat deer study was just a beginning with the Yakama Nation. Going in, I was only guaranteed a three-year job—the life of a short research grant. I accepted that this might be a temporary stop and I'd be job-hunting again before our newborn son was old enough for preschool. But Bill Bradley was a man on a mission, and he and others successfully lobbied for extensions to the grant. A three-year study became a five-year and then a seven-year study. Little did I know when I joined the Yakama Nation's Wildlife Program that I would be there for thirteen years and leave after having acquired a doctoral degree. It was no small season in my career, and my time there had an enormous impact on me—professionally and personally.

Bill continued to work with those who controlled the BIA's purse strings in Washington, DC. The success of the Klickitat deer study helped him make a compelling argument that there was much more to do, and our research grant should be rolled into a permanent funding stream dedicated to large mammal work on the Yakama Reservation. And it worked. It was one piece that allowed Bill to grow a program that in 1985 had a single wildlife biologist, himself, and a habitat biologist—two biologists for a reservation of over a million acres and a ceded territory greater than ten million acres.

I was the first biologist added to fulfill Bill's vision. But within three years, he had secured the means to add an upland bird biologist, a waterfowl and wetlands biologist, a forest wildlife biologist, and a spotted owl biologist, plus a cadre of wildlife technicians to support the diverse work the program was now doing. By the early 1990s, the Yakamas had the largest Native American wildlife program in the country.

Wildlife biologists work for an array of employers, but traditionally, most work for federal and state wildlife management agencies. Others work in places like private consulting firms, government contractors, and non-governmental organizations like the National Wildlife Federation, the National Wild Turkey Federation, and Defenders of Wildlife, among others.

I never considered working as a wildlife biologist for a Native American tribe before Bill called me in 1988. When I showed up in Toppenish on my first day, I had no idea what to expect. It was probably impossible to know without spending time in a Native American community—and I never had. Any work setting is embedded in an underlying human culture. The cultural backdrop where most wildlife biologists traditionally work is similar, even if missions and management philosophies differ. Family and social norms provide the framework around which cultures develop and are nurtured. Native American culture, especially on a reservation, is unique—unlike what most non-Native Americans have ever experienced.

Evidence that Yakama culture was intimately connected to the natural landscape, and the fish and wildlife that had sustained their ancestors for centuries, was prominent in tribal facilities—artwork on the walls, departmental insignias, in the tribal people themselves. Wildlife was not an amenity or simply a source of recreation here—human life itself was dependent on the fish in the rivers and the animals in the forests, wetlands, and prairies. Tribal legends are replete with stories about wildlife, animating moral attributes—the coyote as trickster, for example—even the ontogeny of the landscape itself is steeped in colorful oral traditions.

My work for the Yakama Nation benefitted greatly from the support of tribal leaders and elders—key guardians of the tradition-rich Yakama culture. They knew the work was relevant and important—good wildlife management supported tribal cultural values and treaty rights. Carrol Palmer, director of all Yakama natural resource programs, advocated for the work and the biologist leading it. I was grateful. Tribal elders—people like William Yallup Sr., Jerry Meninick, Levi George, Russell Jim, and Dave Blodgett Sr.—spoke highly of our research and enthusiastically sought updates. Of particular importance to me was another elder, General Council Chairman Phillip "Bing" Olney. For several years during my time with the Yakamas, Bing led the General Council, the body of all enrolled tribal members—the tribe's body politic. This group was different than the Tribal Council, the ruling body of tribal government.

Bing also held a position as a wildlife technician in our program, mostly involved in upland wildlife and wetlands work. He occasionally helped during the later years of my field work. Then in his sixties, Bing was a tough and capable worker. Reliable and trustworthy, he had an unassailable positive attitude and was excited to be on our team. We became good friends. He was a constant source of encouragement, and he always advocated for our work.

By 1993, we had done everything we set out to do in the Klickitat deer research effort and had answered the key questions posed in 1988. It was time to think about what was next. Our grant could now be used for any large mammal work the Yakama Nation believed was important. Bill Bradley was proud of what we accomplished in the Klickitat, and I had earned his trust. He told me that the decision about what to pursue next was mine. We knew a lot about deer now, and the Klickitat population was the largest and most important. We knew far less about Yakama Reservation elk.

There were three primary elk herds on the reservation, defined by where they wintered. The Satus herd was small. It wintered along the eastern extent of forest habitat near Satus Pass and the Satus Creek drainage. The Cedar Valley herd, also small, wintered in the central part of the reservation. The largest herd—the Toppenish Creek herd—wintered in a diverse foothill complex above and west of the developed part of the

An ear-tagged, radio-collared bull elk in a panel trap just prior to release on the Yakama Nation Reservation in January 1998, during the large research study the author led as part of his doctoral work at the University of Montana. | Scott McCorquodale photo.

reservation. Most of its winter range was also within the Toppenish Creek Game Reserve, the only area of the Yakama Reservation designated by tribal resolution as protected winter range for elk and deer. This large area was also off-limits to hunting.

With Bill's blessing, I redirected our research resources to the Toppenish Creek elk herd. I was about to start my second big elk study. We didn't know much about Toppenish Creek elk movements, habitat selection, or demographics. Once more, we needed to get our hands on some elk, and we needed collar data—a lot of it. I had to develop a new capture program. We could dart them from the air, as we had done on the ALE Reserve—and we eventually did some of that—but it was too expensive to rely on helicopter work for the number the elk we needed to collar. Our grant wasn't that large. Plus, this was not all open country like the Hanford Site. We needed other methods. Luckily, there was a flat, forested plateau interspersed with meadows in the heart of the Toppenish herd's winter range—just below a mountain called Deer Butte. The plateau—Kah Mah Singh, as it was known—was accessible by road, sort of. We could get our trucks up in winter sometimes, but we'd likely need snowmobiles when deep snow came. Another appealing feature was that the entire area was behind a locked gate after the first of November. Nobody would be up there but us. It was ideal—the right topography and habitat and a secure trapping area.

We used panel traps—wooden corrals with high walls and a door that elk tripped themselves. We deployed seven panel traps across the plateau. The walls I designed were modular—adjacent walls connected by metal pins and hinges—so the traps could be moved easily, wall by wall. The counterweighted door had a two-piece bailing wire trigger line with a breakaway that ran just in front of an alfalfa bait pile. When an elk tried to get a free meal, it would bump and release the breakaway, and the counterweighted door would slam shut behind it. Using more bailing wire, we anchored the trap walls to at least three or four pine trees to make sure they could withstand the inevitable challenges a trapped elk would give the walls.

Large panel traps could catch groups of elk—a strategy that had been employed elsewhere—but I had research questions that related to both cow and bull elk ecology. Capturing bulls with other elk was dangerous—they would defend their space when stressed in a trap and probably gore other elk. I mitigated this risk by building smaller traps, ones unlikely to catch more than one elk at a time. During summer 1994, my technician and research partner, Dave Blodgett Jr., and I built the corrals in our office parking lot, and they were all in place below Deer Butte by late October. Later, I thought "Elk" Butte would have been a more apt name. We also constructed a pair of larger clover traps—a stretch version of what we had used for the Klickitat deer.

A research-tagged and radio-collared bull elk in a panel trap in December 1995, is about to be released on the Yakama Nation Reservation during a large and lengthy study the author led on elk survival, vulnerability to hunting, and habitat use. | Scott McCorquodale photo.

For six years, we trapped elk each winter on Deer Butte. We waited for the first snowfall—typically about mid-November, and trapped until elk could no longer be enticed with alfalfa—usually about the beginning of March. As I suspected, the access road was challenging at times—we chained up when we had to and worked off snowmobiles when the going got tough. At times, it was a slog up the hill from the gate, but we were good at slogging.

We had been able to handle Klickitat deer without sedation, but that wasn't feasible with the much larger elk in our panel traps. No one on our team was willing to go into the traps and grab a hind leg of an unsedated five-hundred-pound elk. Nor was I keen to try my "open field tackle" approach on an elk. We darted each one in the trap and handled them after they dropped in the hay, and we did it nearly every winter day.

As with deer in the Klickitat, snow was the key to success. The trapping area was high enough that we usually had snow on the ground for about three months. We caught elk nearly every night—usually more than one. There were times when we had elk in all seven of our traps. We also caught a few deer—nothing kept them out. We even caught a

Having been trapped, darted, and radio-collared, a bull elk awakens from sedation in a panel trap just prior to release on the Yakama Nation Reservation in December 1995, during the large, multiyear study the author led while earning his doctorate and working as a research biologist for the Yakama Wildlife Program. | Scott McCorquodale photo.

wandering domestic steer early in the season. Our trap design worked well. In the entire study, we only caught more than a single elk in a trap two or three times.

Darting elk in the traps was a tad tricky. They had enough space to move around—usually pacing rapidly back and forth along the wall opposite to where we stood. Darting a moving animal is not ideal—darts loaded with a drug dose are heavy and have poor ballistics relative to a bullet. The trick was to dart them as they began pivoting to reverse course along the back wall. I pulled the trigger in the middle of the pivot move—the only time they were not moving left to right or vice versa. Timing was everything, and I only missed once. Dave darted elk, too, and I don't remember him ever missing.

On our first morning of trapping, we encountered an elk we came to know well. As we walked into our second trap, I saw that the door was shut and there was movement in the open gaps between the wall boards. I peered in to see a large bull pacing back and forth. Our first capture of the study—and a beautiful animal. I prepared a dart, popped him in the butt with my dart gun, and watched him fall over a few minutes later. We processed and released him as per usual. Before the week was out, we saw him on another morning in a different trap. We didn't need to get our hands on him again, so we just opened the door and freed him.

Over the next five years, we saw him repeatedly. We caught him so often we lost count. In research, we call this a "trap-happy" animal. He quickly learned that the poke in the butt was a one-time thing—first day only. After that, traps were just a free meal and a warm bed of hay for the night.

Over the course of the study, we captured 200 different elk—112 cows and 88 bulls. We caught many of them more than once. The traps worked well. We only had two escapes—one over a wall and one through a wall. We hung radio collars on 81 elk, 52 of them adult bulls. As in the Klickitat, we used ground antenna arrays to radio-track in winter, and I was back in the air weekly spring through fall doing aerial telemetry, usually in a Cessna 182. The era of GPS collars was still in the future, but not far. For now, I had to fly many hours to get the data we needed.

Those data came in at a steady pace, and we worked hard for them. Migration patterns became clearer every year. We accumulated information needed to determine which habitats were most important. Some of the collared elk died, giving us the ability to estimate annual survival rates for bulls and cows—and assess the primary causes of death. Blood samples gave us pregnancy rates, and teeth gave us the ages of the elk we caught. Aerial surveys gave us demographics and elk density. Toppenish herd elk, much like Klickitat deer, were traditional—each went to the same areas for winter and summer every year. Most elk went westward to higher elevations after winter. Some went so far as to technically be in western Washington.

Bing Olney was with us one day when we checked traps, which was not unusual. He was a veteran elk trapper by then. The drug we used to sedate elk worked well, but occasionally they'd reawaken briefly and, on rare occasions, even get back to their feet. This day was one of those occasions. Because of their size, elk are hard to move when they are on the ground—we routinely processed them in the trap, right where they fell. This morning a cow elk we were processing suddenly aroused, and I knew she was getting up. I yelled, "Out" to the three technicians with me in the trap—Bing included. Three of us made it through the door—Bing was fourth in line. His escape was blocked by the woozy but technically awake elk. This was

An ear-tagged, radio-collared bull elk sprints from a panel trap on the Yakama Nation Reservation in January 1998, one of eighty-eight bull elk that were radio-collared and tracked during the multiyear study. | Scott McCorquodale photo.

our only trap with a live tree standing inside it, and Bing instinctively got behind it. We closed the door to prevent the elk's escape because we weren't finished with her, and she still needed a reversal shot.

We knew Bing was safe. The elk was not overtly aggressive—just suspicious of the guy behind the tree. Over the next several minutes there was an amusing standoff between Bing, hands on the tree, and the cow elk peering around the left, then the right as she assessed the threat of this tribal elder. They were maybe five feet apart. Bing was light on his feet for a sixty-something guy, dancing back and forth to match the elk's every move. I never feared he'd be injured—the tree was an effective shield. I soon darted her a second time, with a light dose, and she went back down quickly. Bing's poker game with a live elk in a trap became a legend of sorts in our program—a legend that usually generated laughter with each retelling.

After a couple years, it was clear that our effort was successful. We were learning things nobody knew before about these elk—in some cases about elk in general—unraveling more wildlife secrets. We gained a good understanding of the migration patterns of these elk, which had been unknown before our study. They wintered on the reservation, but many migrated to summer ranges on national forestlands to the west. We also found that bulls migrated to winter range earlier than cows. This was at odds with the common thinking among elk managers, but elk migration had rarely been evaluated with real data such as we had. Once the rut ended, the fat-depleted adult bulls didn't wait for big snows but headed for winter foraging areas before the big herds came down. This was clearly adaptive. If they waited too long, they might have to tread many miles through deep snow, and that would take energy. Post-rut, they had no extra energy to spare.

Half of our radio-collared elk died during the study—more bulls than cows. Annual survival for bulls was 65 percent—for cows it was 83 percent. Most deaths were from hunting, but not all. Elk, mostly old ones, also died from starvation in winter; cougars killed a small number. The trap-happy bull that was our first capture of the study died of old age—just before his eighteenth birthday. Most collared elk killed by people died between late August and late October on summer–fall ranges. We found that the presence and density of open roads and the complexity of the terrain on these ranges provided a good predictor of the risk to elk from hunters. Rough country and less road access deterred hunting.

I had one other objective—to develop a tool that would help estimate elk numbers from aerial survey data when all the elk could not be seen, which was always the case. Some colleagues in Idaho had developed sightability correction models by now. These mathematical models used data such as how many elk are in a group and how much tree cover exists to estimate a formal probability that the group would be seen from a helicopter—the key to an estimate of how many elk were missed during the survey. This approach is not unlike the model my doctor uses

A large, ear-tagged and radio-collared bull elk, still a bit groggy shortly after being released by the author's research team in the Toppenish Creek Game Reserve on the Yakama Nation Reservation in January 1996. This work led to the author's doctorate from the University of Montana. | Scott McCorquodale photo.

at my annual physical when he inputs my age, cholesterol, blood pressure, family occurrence of heart disease, and so on to estimate my risk of a heart attack in the coming year and decide whether I need statins or some other medication. The math is the same. With sightability models, we are estimating the chances (or risk) of an elk group being sighted based on factors we can measure—factors that affect seeing versus not seeing them.

So far, researchers had developed all sightability models based on data from cow elk only. But bull elk and cows are different in many ways. In winter, when most surveys are undertaken, bulls are in smaller groups than cows, have more affinity for cover, use areas of deeper snow, and are even slightly different in color—their torsos are blonder. Wildlife biologists assumed that a model developed from cow elk data worked fine for bulls. I wanted to test that and, if needed, build a model that accounted for gender differences. Our study population had a robust bull subpopulation, and we had many bulls collared—a requisite for building any model.

Bill had been watching our progress, had seen this horse run before—the large mammal research team consisting of me and my primary technician. He knew we had another good study going, and he approached me one day with a proposal. The work we were doing was complex, and we were going to have excellent datasets. He fully expected we'd have publishable results. He asked me what I thought about using the elk study as a PhD project for myself? I didn't expect that question, and I immediately saw obstacles. Kim and I now had three children—in seventh, fourth, and first grades. How would this work? Was I even up to the challenge of a doctoral program at this stage of life? Most universities require some extended period on campus—how would that be possible?

I didn't think Kim would have much enthusiasm for Bill's proposal, but I was wrong. She liked the idea and thought it would open even more jobs for me in the future, which was good for the family. She even thought that if we needed to spend a season somewhere else near a university, the "team" would be up for it. Bill and Kim were totally on board, while I was waffling. But they were convincing, so I started investigating how it might work. In all honesty, I remained skeptical.

Over a period of weeks, I contacted faculty members I still knew at the University of Montana. I had a fully funded project underway—that was appealing to them and unusual for a prospective student. The university in Missoula required only one academic year on campus. Meanwhile, Bill worked on the possibility of a leave of absence of sorts. Eventually, he convinced the tribal leaders to let me be away for nine months—an academic year. I'd work on some assignments for the program from Missoula and still receive a half salary. The university would provide a funded fellowship that made up the other half. It all came together. By the time I left the employ of the Yakama Nation a few years later, I had the designation "Ph.D." after my name. It was a remarkable and totally unforeseen outcome of my time there.

The Toppenish Creek elk study supported my successful doctoral program, and I authored several papers in scientific journals. I gained a great deal of knowledge and experience, and the Yakama Nation now knew much more about the Toppenish herd. Along the way, Dave Blodgett Jr. and I also started a black bear study on the reservation, but that's a whole other chapter. We worked on the elk study and the bear study at the same time—two studies at once, by a full-time team of just two people. The major field seasons for bear and elk work were different—we trapped elk in winter when bears were asleep, and trapped bears in summer, when I mostly piled up elk data from weekly flights. We were busy, and we accomplished a great deal. And I had a ton of fun—so did Dave.

In summer 2001, I received another unexpected phone call that changed our lives again. It was from another Dave—Assistant Director Dave Brittell, in charge of the WDFW's Wildlife Program. I'd met Dave but didn't know him well. He was a good friend of Bill Bradley's, though. Dave said the agency had a job opening coming up—the statewide research lead for elk and deer—and he hoped I might consider applying for it. I was a bit surprised—unaware that Dave had been tracking our work with deer in the Klickitat and elk in Toppenish Creek. There was another big conversation coming for Kim and me.

The job Dave Brittell pitched me was a terrific opportunity. It would come with even more resources than my job at the Yakama Nation. I'd also have access to a larger team and work statewide with a host of bright and dedicated district biologists from the Pacific Coast to the Idaho border. There was one more key element—it was a statewide job, but they wanted the person stationed mid-state, in Yakima or Ellensburg. If I got the job, my family wouldn't have to move. We could live in our house in Selah, just north of Yakima.

It seemed like the right time and the right job, but it was difficult to leave my colleagues and friends at the Yakama Nation. The work environment there was as close-knit as I've ever experienced. It felt like home. But sometimes, to keep growing, a person must leave home.

I applied for the state government position of deer and elk specialist, interviewed for it, and was hired. Jerry Nelson, manager of the WDFW Wildlife Program's Deer and Elk Section, chose me among the other candidates and would supervise my work. He, too, was new to the agency.

It was September 2001. I had a new partner and advocate. I knew I was ready, and Jerry knew it too. We formed a productive and enjoyable collaboration that lasted over a decade. We got to know each other well and became close friends. The work we did together was challenging, diverse, and important.

A life is comprised of seasons. My season with the Yakama Nation—thirteen years—was monumental for me and for my family. I grew professionally while doing critical work for the tribe. My skills matured and became more diverse. It was a unique place to work, different from anything before or since. I worked with incredible, passionate people—some Yakama tribal members, some non-Native Americans like me. Although our backgrounds were dissimilar, we shared a common mission. I learned a great deal about a culture deeply integrated with the natural world. Tribal perspectives—about things like time, family, community, the Earth—were different from my own. I grew personally through my relationships with Yakama members—they made me a better person. Most were kind and welcoming. Many I'll never forget. I came for a temporary, three-year job and stayed almost five times longer. It was a remarkable season, and it prepared me well for the next.

Chapter 5

Among Wild Bears

Some Native American cultures evoke the concept of a spirit animal—an innate connection that exists between an animal and a person. If I have a spirit animal, I'm pretty sure it's a grizzly bear. I was probably six or seven when I first saw photographs of scientists John and Frank Craighead working with Yellowstone's wild grizzlies in the pages of *National Geographic*. I think that was the day I became totally enthralled with bears in general and grizzlies in particular. These massive, muscular carnivores can move a five-hundred-pound rock effortlessly, dismember a bison carcass like it's made of Play-Doh, and sprint short distances at thirty-five miles an hour—nearly as fast as a thoroughbred racehorse.

Grizzlies are enduring icons of vast wild places in western North America. They are intimidating, powerful, intelligent creatures, yet they mostly live a peaceful life eating berries, digging roots, and grazing in sedge meadows. Many denizens of the ecosystem coexist peacefully with grizzlies every day. The bears are an enigma. Sure, they kill things from time to time, but they are not obligate carnivores. They can survive eating mostly at the salad bar. Their reputation is well-earned but outsized, given the normal daily life of wild grizzlies.

Though I've seen many since, I didn't see my first wild grizzly until I was in college. I've watched them swimming across alpine lakes, gobbling huckleberries like a Shop-Vac, playing gently with their cubs, and trying—unsuccessfully—to catch a mountain goat. I've seen them ambling across a meadow as the day waned, the soft light just before sunset flashing stunningly across their silver-tipped backs as their powerful muscles rippled with every stride. I've never lost that fascination I first felt for grizzlies as a child with a *National Geographic* in my lap.

When I applied to the undergraduate Wildlife Biology Program at the University of Montana, I was still thinking about grizzly bears, and I aspired to become a grizzly bear biologist when I enrolled the following fall. John Craighead was no longer there, and the Craigheads' Yellowstone study had ended—replaced by a new effort called the Interagency Grizzly Bear Study Team. I learned quickly, however, that there was another large grizzly research program operating out of UM in fall 1979—the Border Grizzly Project (BGP).

Professor and bear expert Chuck Jonkel ran the BGP, which was focused on a large area of northwestern Montana adjacent to the Canadian border. From nearly my first week on campus, I was committed to finding a way into the BGP. Fortunately, Chuck was approachable, so when I asked him about any opportunities for an on-campus student volunteer to do something—anything—useful for the study team, he was accommodating. He walked me down to the BGP bullpen, introduced me to several of the field biologists, and said, "Scott would like to help us—please find things for him to do." It was really that easy.

The people I met in the bullpen were many of the "who's who" in western Montana's grizzly bear world. There was Rick Mace, who went on to spend his entire career studying grizzlies in Montana, and Chris Servheen, who became the first national recovery leader for grizzly bears in the US a few years later. At the time, Chris was finishing his doctoral study of grizzlies in Montana's Mission Mountains. Also on hand was Tim Their, who constantly shared what he knew about bears and how to study them. He was one of the nicest people I ever met in the wildlife biology world. I later met Dan Carney, a skilled grizzly field biologist; Harry Carriles, who was studying interactions between grizzlies and black bears in northwestern Montana; and Mark Haroldson, who became a leader of the Interagency Grizzly Bear Study Team in Yellowstone.

To use a technical term, I was a flunky—but I had access to a grizzly bear research study, and that was enough for me. I did whatever the team needed that could be done in the Missoula office—ran errands, put gas in field trucks, built snares used to trap bears in the research effort, and cleaned and maintained field gear. And I asked questions—lots and lots of questions. I was not getting academic credits for my time in the bullpen; nonetheless, I was in and out of the bullpen multiple times every day, learning valuable lessons.

My first break came on a day when Chuck Jonkel told me he was headed to Kalispell the next day to handle two yearling grizzly bears prior to their release in the Cabinet-Yaak Ecosystem in northwestern Montana. Their mother had been killed, but the yearlings still had a chance to live in the wild. I asked Chuck if he was going alone, and he said he was. Seeing my chance, I asked—without hesitation—if he wanted help. He smiled and told me to meet him at six the next morning. I was going to touch my first wild grizzlies—I barely slept that night.

The drive to Kalispell was just over two hours each way. I was on cloud nine the whole time. I watched Chuck sedate the two young grizzlies, and he let me help tag and collar them. He was gracious as always while I picked his brain about bears for nearly four hours in the truck that day.

I continued to do whatever I could in the BGP bullpen to feel a part of the team and learn more about bears. My next break came when Chuck agreed to let me spend part of summer 1981—just after my junior year—at the Montana-Canada border, helping BGP field crews in the North Fork Flathead River area. I wasn't on the payroll, but I got free meals and lodging in the project cabin, and I logged valuable field time. This was my first experience in the field working on wildlife research.

July 2000 photo of the author with a sedated, nearly five-hundred-pound male black bear sporting a new radio collar. The bear, nicknamed "Charger" for his aggressiveness in the foot snare in which he was captured, was one of 150 different individuals trapped and either radio-collared or tagged on the Yakama Nation Reservation during the study. | D. Blodgett photo.

Originally, I was assigned to assist Harry Carriles. A week later, I had my first experience helping with a bear field capture—of a black bear—in the North Fork. My second capture, again a black bear, came a couple days after that. At the time, another BGP study was in progress just north of the border—on the Canadian side—led by Bruce McLellan, a Canadian doing his University of British Columbia doctoral research on grizzlies in the southeastern part of the province. His primary assistant was veteran grizzly biologist Dan Carney. Shortly after I arrived to join the team, word came that the crew on a third study—a new effort on the Blackfeet Indian Reservation—was having trouble capturing its first grizzlies. Chuck asked Dan, who had a well-earned reputation as an excellent grizzly trapper, to go help the Blackfeet team. He told me to fill in for Dan as Bruce's primary assistant. For a new guy, this was an unbelievable opportunity, and I was thrilled.

Bruce was an incredible mentor—smart, patient, thorough—and his field savvy was excellent. We radio-tracked grizzlies and visited dens of collared bears from the previous winter. I accompanied Bruce on my first-ever tracking flight; and as a means of gathering valuable food habits data, we regularly searched for scat where radio-collared bears had recently wandered. This last element yielded an amazing experience that is still vivid in my memory over forty years later.

For days, Bruce and I had been monitoring a collared female grizzly in Cabin Creek, British Columbia, as she roamed around an old burn covered now with a variety of shrubs that produced preferred grizzly foods. One morning, we checked for her signal in the burn area and found she had finally moved on. This was our chance to do what we had done several times before—beat the brush on foot to find her recent scats. Ironically, as we prepared to start, I asked Bruce if the team ever unexpectedly ran into other bears when going into places that were clearly attractive to collared bears. He couldn't remember that happening.

We packed our rucksacks with poop collecting gear—rubber gloves, sample bags, and Magic Markers. To maximize our effort, Bruce said, we would walk different routes and meet back at the truck in an hour. He pointed me in one direction, then walked off in another. I wandered around, keenly searching the ground for fresh grizzly poo. I found several piles and dutifully bagged samples—not the most elegant field work but interesting for an aspiring bear researcher. Watching the time, I eventually started to amble back up the hill toward the road, planning to meet Bruce again right at his one-hour mark.

As I neared the road, lugging my pack of scat samples, I saw a few smallish trees along the road cut—the only trees standing in the burn. I was just feet below the road surface when I heard footsteps on the gravel above me—Bruce had apparently beaten me back. As I stepped toward a gap in the trees, expecting to see Bruce, the front half of a large grizzly bear suddenly appeared about thirty feet in front of me—almost spitting distance—as it went up on its hind legs to get a better look. We each realized in the same instant what kind of creature the other was.

Staring at me intently, it was a beautiful bear—and it seemed huge. I could see every detail in its steely brown eyes, the texture of its fur, its muscular build. As fear gripped me, my knees seemed made of rubber and adrenaline flooded my heart. I knew I was too close—way too close—and the next few seconds would determine my fate. I took two steps backward—as if that would be enough to make a difference—but it was what I could do.

When in a jam with a grizzly, the advice is always, "Climb a tree if you can, and climb high." The only trees were between me and the bear—no way I was going to move toward it. A second later, the bear dropped down on all fours, disappearing from my view. It was still there, unseen now, but only two charging bear strides away. I waited to hear the brush in front of me exploding with enraged grizzly. What I heard instead was the bear passing through the shrubs on the other side of the road, then silence. It had retreated. In all honesty, I was shocked. At that distance, from what I knew, a surprised grizzly would charge more often than not.

I took a deep breath, then yelled downhill at the top of my lungs, "BRUUUUCE!" No more than a minute later, Bruce appeared below me, hustling up the slope. Apparently, my bellowing of his name contained more information than I thought. He knew something alarming had happened. After I explained what had just occurred, we walked up onto the road. Bruce took a serpentine path on the road, peering here and there, finally kneeling in the dirt to look at something. He waved me over, pointed at the ground, and asked me what I saw. My seeing, hearing, and most other higher neural processes were still garbled by the seeing my life pass before my eyes thing, so I just shrugged my shoulders. "Those are cub claw marks," he said. "This was a sow with babies."

We both went from thinking I had been lucky to thinking I had been ridiculously lucky—a thirty-foot surprise encounter with a mother grizzly and cubs of the year, and not a scratch on me—nothing short of unbelievable. My heart rate didn't return to normal for half an hour. We learned later that day from some loggers that they had recently and repeatedly seen a large, uncollared female grizzly with two cubs in the area. The rest of my time with Bruce was interesting but far less dramatic. I learned a great deal from him and went home with new skills, amazing memories, and one incredible story. I was a little tired of Spam and beans, though.

I am still thankful for the personal growth I experienced during my time in the Flathead River area with Bruce—one more person who helped me on my journey. I finished my degree the following year and began the search for a master's degree opportunity. I was still interested in bears, but I mostly needed to find the right project at a quality university. As happens sometimes, life presented me with a slightly different but equally interesting path. I ended up agreeing to pursue my master's degree at the University of Washington by doing innovative research on some unique elk. For the next fifteen years, I was primarily an ungulate (even-toed, hoofed mammal) researcher, but bears eventually came back into my world.

By 1994, I had finished my master's degree and joined the Yakama Nation Wildlife Program, first doing black-tailed deer research, then starting another elk study. As I roamed the Yakama Reservation with Dave Blodgett Jr., compiling elk study data, I began to notice that we were seeing an awful lot of black bears. We commonly saw multiple bears during late spring aerial surveys for elk. We often saw bears cross the road in front of our trucks. In the fall, we saw so many bear scats in the oaks that it was sometimes an obstacle course to avoid stepping in them. I never saw so many bears or their sign anywhere, national parks included.

No one knew much about the biology of reservation bears, except that they were abundant. Linguists have debated the best derivation of the name "Yakama," but many believe it translates to "black bear." Clearly, bears are an important animal in the tribe's cultural traditions. Tribal members hunt deer and elk passionately, but few are inclined to shoot a bear. For many, there is a cultural taboo—the bear is the brother of man. For others, bears are just not preferred table fare.

In February 1998, a radio-collared female black bear stares down at the author from her winter den, a large cavity fifty feet off the ground in a live Douglas fir on the Yakama Nation Reservation. Bears on the reservation used a variety of sites for their winter dens, but not many denned high in live trees. | Scott McCorquodale photo.

I had a background with bears and experience trapping and handling them. I grew increasingly curious about the reservation's bear population and finally approached Bill Bradley with the idea of trying to learn more about these bears through research. If it didn't impact our ongoing elk work, he was all for it. I was confident that Dave and I could juggle things and work on elk and bears at the same time. We could pool gear and telemetry flight time for two efforts—more bang for the buck.

I enlisted a local welder to fabricate several portable bear culvert traps and purchased everything we needed to start building bear snares. These consisted of a loop of quarter-inch galvanized aircraft cable with an angle-iron slide attached to a tree or drag log by a similar length of cable. An industrial swivel connected the foot snare cable to the anchor tree cable, preventing twisting by a trapped bear, and a heavy metal spring triggered the snare loop. Field teams often referred to the entire assembly as an Aldrich foot snare. Used properly, a foot snare is a humane and effective way to catch bears for research. They were the primary capture tool for many bear studies, including the Border Grizzly Project. We were about to add bear trapping to our repertoire.

We trapped our first bear on a beautiful day in late May on upper Toppenish Creek—a young adult female. Bears breed mostly in June, but females can enter estrus anytime between late May and early July. As I prepared to dart our snared bear, I noticed on the bald toe of a forested hill about fifty yards away a large black bear sitting on its haunches like a dog, watching us intently. I knew right away that it was our bear's consort—they were bear-dating, so to speak. The entire time we spent with our bear—tagging, collaring, and the like—the attentive male sat motionless on the hill, watching our goings-on with his intended mate. It was not the last time we dealt with a free-ranging consort at the capture site of a snared female.

We typically deployed snares in the woods in what biologists refer to as a "cubby set"—a snare attached to a single tree, with logs piled up against the anchor tree on two sides, their ends crisscrossed behind the tree, creating a one-way opening to a bait at the base of the anchor tree. Then we buried the snare at the entrance, directly in front of the bait. We set cubbies all the time and caught lots of bears in them. We continually fine-tuned our cubby sets and became experts at fooling bears with variations on the basic set. We typically crisscrossed sticks on the ground at the cubby entrance to guide a bear's steps into the set. Bears normally preferred to step onto bare ground between sticks rather than on the sticks. With practice, we could often predict which front foot the snare would catch—always a front foot. We usually caught at least a bear a week, often more. We set a record when we caught eleven bears in one night with twelve active trap sites—a mixture of culvert traps and snare sets. Like I said, there were many bears on the reservation—more than anywhere else I'd been.

The morning was bright, the sky clear—spring wildflowers were in full bloom. As Dave and I drove up the road to one of our cubbies, we wondered if our luck had changed. We had been toying with one particularly

On the Yakama Nation Reservation in June 1996, an adult female black bear snagged in a research snare climbs the tree to which the snare is anchored while the sedative from the dart in her shoulder takes effect and allows the author to safely attach a radio collar. Typically, a sedated bear will be awake and mobile again in about an hour. | Scott McCorquodale photo.

careful bear at the next cubby for nearly a week. She found our lure site before we ever set a snare—that was our usual process—a smelly lure poured on a stump or log in hope of attracting a bear. Once we had a bear's interest, we either set a snare or pulled in a portable culvert trap. One of our favorite lures was old grill grease we obtained by the bucket-load from a local burger joint. This smelly goo was irresistible to bears. After we first set the trap at the site ahead of us that day, the bear came back three nights in a row, and we missed her each night. Wary of the opening to the bait, she triggered the snare without getting caught the first night, then pulled down one side of the cubby the next two nights, stealing our bait of fry-grease-covered apples each time.

We had her locked into this set though. We saw her running away once, and we nicknamed her "Greasy," in honor of her interest in fry grease. Bears are very smart. Sometimes it is a battle of wits to catch a wary one. The night before—our fourth try at Greasy—we threw her a curveball. She had entered through the cubby wall on the same side both

A female black bear nicknamed "Greasy" awakens from sedation with a new radio collar after being trapped on the Yakama Nation Reservation by the author and his research assistant, Dave Blodgett Jr., in May 1995. It took several nights to outsmart this particular bear, who kept eluding capture in a trap baited with grease-covered apples. | Scott McCorquodale photo.

previous nights. Our curveball was that there was no snare at the mouth of the cubby this time—it just looked like there was. The snare was buried just outside the wall she kept pulling down.

As we parked and started walking through the lodgepole pines to the cubby, we heard the vocalization—a kind of bear wail that was common to trapped bears. Then we saw her through the trees, bouncing around and pulling the foot that was attached to the anchor tree by a length of aircraft cable. Greasy was a great fastball-over-the-plate hitter, but the curveball got her. Dave and I high-fived and prepared to collar another bear.

We used a hodgepodge of things as bear bait—whatever we could get. Attractive bait is key to trapping success. The fry-grease-covered apples worked great. So did road-killed deer or meaty beef bones from the local rendering plant. But the best bait was something we accidentally concocted during a warm spell. The tribal fisheries program sometimes gave us hatchery salmon or steelhead that had been vacuum-packed and kept in cold storage for tribal members' needs. When the vacuum seals failed

In June 1996, an adult female black bear snagged in a research snare keeps her eyes on the author while the sedative from the darts in her hip takes effect and allows the author to safely attach a radio collar around her neck. The first dart did not work properly, necessitating a second. | Scott McCorquodale photo.

and the fish were no longer suitable for table fare, the fish came our way. We kept five-gallon buckets of fish chunks in our truck beds, letting them ripen. We discovered that if the fish sat in the bucket for a few days during warm weather, it liquified into a gooey, gag-reflex-inducing gruel. It was repulsive to people, but olfactory motivated bears loved it. We didn't use it in the culverts—too messy—but we often used it at snares, pouring it into a small bucket at the base of the anchor tree. The trick was to not get any on our clothes while setting the cubby. No amount of laundering could get that smell out.

We trapped from about mid-April to the end of July most years, avoiding hot weather. Sometimes we trapped again for a few weeks in the autumn. I had one of my most amazing experiences with bears one fall. A television news reporter called me one day in September. He'd heard about our project and was interested in doing a story for the evening news. It so happened that we had recently retrieved a collar from a dead elk and were trying to redeploy it on a bear before winter. I told the reporter we had a few traps set but couldn't guarantee anything. He said

In June 1996, a large male black bear sits against a tree with a research snare attached to one front foot. From a few feet away, the author is about to use an air pistol to shoot a drug-laden dart into the bear to sedate it for safe handling. | Scott McCorquodale photo.

he could make a story, even if he just filmed us with an antenna, listening to a radio-collared bear. I replied that we would try to let him cover a capture before we settled for that version—if he could be ready to go at a moment's notice. He agreed.

A couple days later, I checked a culvert trap at a promising site and had a bear. I immediately drove to a nearby high point to call the reporter. I was more comfortable waiting with a bear in a culvert than in a snare, but I told him, "I need you here in thirty minutes." He arrived in twenty-five. I briefly gave him the plan, then we walked to the trap, which was visible from our parking spot. It looked like a subadult bear, one we had never caught before. The reporter was already filming when I put a dart into the air pistol. After darting the bear, I told the reporter the drugs would work better it we stepped away and didn't stare at the bear the whole time. After he set his tripod on the ground, we backed off about eight feet and knelt quietly, waiting for our bear to drift off to sleep. The reporter still had the camera on his shoulder.

Within thirty seconds of our stepping back, another bear suddenly emerged from the brush near the trap and began poking curiously at the tripod on the ground. The astonished look on the reporter's face was priceless. The new bear could clearly see us and eventually started to act fidgety. I had enough experience with bears by now to be good at reading their body language. I told the reporter I thought I could tree this bear for him to film. As the bear glanced away for an escape route, I jumped up and ran toward it, clapping my hands and yelling, "Hey bear, hey bear!" The startled bear immediately took flight, running around the edge of a tangle of shrubs. As I clapped and yelled, following the bear, a different bear shot up a tree six feet to my left—bear number three. The reporter filmed the treed bear briefly, then I suggested we check on our trapped bear, which should be down by now.

As we rounded the shrubs again to approach the trap, I looked past it and saw another bear ambling toward us through the trees—bear number four. I treed that one, too, and the reporter got more film footage. We returned to find our sleeping bear in the trap. I didn't collar it because it was not quite an adult, but I did tag it and give it a lip tattoo—standard practice. A few minutes later, it staggered off into the oaks.

Still needing a bear to collar, I reset the trap for the night, and the reporter and I walked the forty yards back to my truck. I debriefed the amazed reporter—his back now toward the trap. While answering his questions, I looked past him to see another bear approaching the trap I just reset. We both watched as the bear entered the trap and the door slammed shut—bear number five. Running back to the trap, I saw it was another subadult bear—one we had already tagged—so I opened the door and restored its freedom. I knew there were a lot of bears on the reservation, but that day surprised even me. The reporter who once was going to settle for a biologist waving an antenna around, filmed five wild bears at close range in about an hour. I can only imagine what he told his colleagues when he got back to the station.

That site was in an oak flat along Toppenish Creek. It was a good acorn year, and bear scats resembling pumpkin pie filling littered the flat. The bears were eating almost nothing but acorns. The profusion of bears that day with the reporter was unusual, but it gave further evidence that the reservation's bear habitat was excellent and the distribution of key foods—like acorns and huckleberries higher in the forest—could yield extraordinarily high seasonal bear densities.

A large, sedated male black bear on the Yakama Reservation wears a new radio collar placed by the author in July 2000. This bear weighed well over four hundred pounds in late summer and probably added another fifty to one hundred pounds during fall foraging before denning for the winter. | Scott McCorquodale photo.

There were more amazing bears experiences to come. One occurred while we were studying elk, not bears. After we got our first good dump of snow one November, we prepped for winter elk trapping by pre-baiting for about a week before setting our traps—a common tactic. The morning after setting the traps, we began rolling up the hill in our trucks, driving in the wheel ruts we'd created over the past few days in eight inches of new snow. Halfway up the hill to the traps, I noticed a fresh set of tracks crossing the road—probably elk, I thought. As I drove over the tracks, I rolled down my window and was immediately surprised—not elk, but bear. It should be asleep in a den somewhere.

When we reached the second elk panel trap, I saw fresh bear tracks in the snow again as I walked toward the trap. Its door was shut, which usually meant we had caught something—hopefully an elk. Then I noticed an ominous sign—blood-smeared snow in a drag mark under the bottom edge of the trap door. Inside the empty trap we found more blood—a lot more—and deer tracks. Following the bloody drag mark out the door, we found the dead deer twenty yards away in the pine stand adjacent to the elk trap, its partly eaten carcass covered in snow.

A young male black bear nicknamed "Blondie" awakens from field sedation by the author on the Yakama Nation Reservation in May 1995. Blondie was trapped in a research snare, but because of his youth and anticipated rapid growth over the next year, he was not given a radio collar. He was ear-tagged to create a history should he be encountered again. | Scott McCorquodale photo.

Over the next week, the bear found all our elk traps and was running the trapline every day, just like we were. If a trap held an elk, he went to the next trap. If he found a deer, he went in after another meal. Smart bear. He clearly knew his weight class. We knew we had to deal with the bear, so we suspended elk trapping and set a culvert trap. He was trap savvy and avoided the trigger in the culvert when he stole the bait—part of one of his two deer kills.

Impatient to get back to elk trapping, I set a snare. I hadn't done that in snow before, but we caught him the first night the snare was set. I drugged, hobbled, and ear-tagged him, and we put him in the bed of my pickup. Dave and I then drove him up the one plowed road that went to higher elevations of the reservation. After several miles and a thousand-foot elevation gain, we chained up and churned our way a small distance up an unplowed road. There, we released the bear. I hoped his only good option would be to locate a den. We didn't see him again that winter. Interestingly, he was back on the elk trapline the next winter. Déjà vu all over again.

I'll say it again—bears are very smart—the closest thing to people running around in the woods. My apologies to the bigfoot fans. Field work on bears was always interesting. We trapped about 150 different bears on the reservation, and we caught several more than once, like the skinny, awkward yearling—the Beaver—and his mom, Mrs. Cleaver. We attached radio collars to sixty-one bears. With the recaptures, we handled Yakama Reservation black bears about two hundred times. We nicknamed more bears than we ever did deer and elk. Many were descriptive, like the stocky male with short legs and broad head—Tank; the male with seemingly oversized forearms—Popeye; a cream-colored one—Blondie; the old sow—Granny; the one-testicle male—Uno; and the aggressive and combative male—Rambo.

Trapping bears was exciting, and we spent more time pondering how to outsmart them than we did deer and elk. Their intellect made them challenging to catch, and that made it fun. I think we eventually captured every bear that made repeated visits to a lure site or snare. Approaching a wild bear moving around in a snare and getting close enough to dart it with a carbon dioxide (CO_2) pistol—our usual tool—was a rush. We had to get within fifteen to twenty feet. Surprisingly, even at that close range, black bears were usually remarkably nonaggressive. They'd pull the snare cable to its limit, away from where we stood, or climb the trunk of the tree that anchored the snare.

But there were exceptions. A nearly five-hundred-pound male we aptly named Charger was theatrical, with aggressive lunges and a back-flip or two. A male we dubbed Rodman essentially pulled the snare cable taught, then ran laps around the anchor tree, taking a swing at me with his free foreleg every time the circle brought him in my direction. A plethora of wounds on his head from breeding season fights helped earn him his nickname. Those and the yellow antiseptic spray with which we treated each wound left him looking like he'd had his hair fashionably dyed. Bears in culverts often hissed, huffed, and jaw-popped at us when we were darting them. Snared bears did that, too, but less often.

Occasionally, I brought Kim or the kids when we checked traps. One day, with my eight-year-old daughter Katie along, we handled two bears in snares on a gorgeous late spring day. One bear was a beautiful adult female in her prime. The entire time we processed her, two tiny cubs of the year watched from a large tree branch about fifteen feet above our heads. The cubs neither moved nor made a sound—mom had put them in stealth mode, and they were good at it. My daughter was thrilled—a perk of having a research biologist dad. I was thrilled that she was thrilled. It was exciting to share these experiences with my family. They saw things most people never do.

Confusing to some, black bears are not always black. In the West, variations are common. We captured black, black bears, but also bears that were deep brown, light brown, reddish, almost yellow, and cream-colored. The truly black individuals were the minority. One bear we snared, a large male we called Rocky, had a light salt and pepper back and dark chocolate brown legs and head. Sitting next to him, I could see how someone might think this almost five-hundred-pound bear was a grizzly, but he wasn't. He was, however, one of the prettiest black bears I've ever seen.

One of the most interesting things about temperate zone bears is their winter sleep. Scientists have long debated whether bears are true hibernators, like ground squirrels, or just deeply lethargic in their dens. I've been to many dens of collared bears and peered inside. I've never seen a denned bear that didn't awaken and look at me, but they were all extremely torpid and nonaggressive. Early in the denning period, they are more arousable and, if disturbed, may flee the den. I've seen such bears abandon a den and reestablish a new one. As a rule, we did not visit dens until midwinter, and none of those bears ever vacated a den.

We tracked collared bears to many types of dens. Most common were hollow logs or areas excavated under stumps or the root balls of fallen trees. But we found bear dens in caves, rockslides, and holes in the ground; in stacks of unused logs left in logging areas, hollow cavities way up live trees, and under the decks of rural cabins. Most unusual was the male bear we found denned miles into the treeless shrub-steppe—a simple nest beneath an overhanging shrub in a shallow draw. He did this in two consecutive years.

Visiting dens in winter was a process. First, I located the den of a collared bear by tracking it in an airplane—the signals transmitted from dens well. With a good fix on a den's location, the visit required driving as close as possible in four-wheel-drive trucks, tires often chained on unplowed roads. Then we pulled snowmobiles out of the trucks for a few more miles of breaking trail in deep snow. Finally came the strenuous snowshoe hike. A GPS unit with the coordinates from the plane got us close, and then we used a handheld antenna and receiver to track the bear to its winter abode. We were good at spotting the telltale signs of a den site once we got within a hundred yards—fallen logs, downed trees with attached root balls, rock walls with large cracks.

Cubs are born in winter dens in January or February. While mom sleeps, the tiny cubs—about the size of a stick of butter at birth—nurse frequently, making an odd buzzing sound easily heard outside the den. Mother black bears emerge in late March or early April with their tiny cubs in tow. They forego breeding and spend the rest of the summer and fall teaching their babies how to be bears. They all den together again the next winter and emerge in spring when the cubs are just over a year old. The yearlings become independent that summer, and mom breeds again. Grizzly moms often skip a second year of breeding and den again with their yearling cubs.

Dens provided us an opportunity to recapture radio-collared bears for checkups or resize collars as bears matured or batteries neared expiration. We occasionally handled denned bears for such reasons. Not all dens provided good opportunities, but many did. Bears in dens still needed sedation—they were never lethargic enough for us to enter safely without the drugs.

One den recapture was especially memorable. We had originally snared Popeye in the summer as a still-growing adult male. He was beautiful—jet black and muscular—and weighed a bit under three hundred pounds. Two winters later, I thought we should visit his den—I suspected he had grown substantially, and his collar had not fallen off as we expected. We tracked him to a den excavated below a large tree stump on the northern flank of Signal Peak, deep in the reservation's mountains. As I shined a flashlight into the den entrance, he awoke and peered out at me groggily. His collar appeared tight but not yet creating any genuine problem. I decided we would come back in a few days and remove the collar.

I returned the next week with Dave and another staff biologist who wanted to observe. Popeye was still in his den—and he looked huge. I prepared a drug-laden dart and popped him in the shoulder with the CO_2 pistol. After several minutes, he appeared glassy-eyed. To be sure he was ready for visitors in his den, I took a nearby piece of wood and poked him gently. He made a dramatic lunge at the branch with his front legs and let out a loud "WOOF." Clearly, he wasn't ready. Ten minutes later, though, he was unresponsive to stimuli.

I leaned into the den entrance and tied a rope to his collar for leverage because his mass was going to make the rest challenging. Though the entrance was cramped, two of us grabbed his front legs and another pulled the rope. We barely moved him a short distance, and it was clear we couldn't get him completely out of the den. After a couple more strenuous pulls, we had his massive head and neck at the entrance where we could access the collar adequately enough to remove it. I had already decided he would not get another. We learned what we needed to from Popeye. After today, the only evidence of our contact with him would be the small ear tags and his lip tattoo. Popeye weighed at least five hundred pounds now. I wished him a good life as we pushed him back into his den and began our trek downhill in the snow to the trucks below.

My dream job had once been to study wild grizzlies. I had a chance to do that—briefly. I am grateful for the opportunity Chuck Jonkel gave me and for all I learned from the Border Grizzly Project team, especially from Bruce McLellan. My path led mostly in a different direction after that—with wild ungulates—an alternative dream job. I never lost my fascination with bears, though, and I'm grateful that I was able to study wild bears in another season of my life. Grizzlies are probably still my spirit animal, but black bears are pretty darn cool, too.

Chapter 6

The Flying

"There she is." "Chirp, chirp, chirp…." The voice on the helicopter's intercom belonged to Jess Hagerman, our exceptional wildlife capture pilot. The audible electronic "chirps" were emanating from a GPS-equipped collar around the neck of a female elk somewhere below and ahead of us. The mission was a familiar one. Locate a series of elk wearing the GPS collars we had deployed a year or two earlier. Each collar contained a bounty of sequential location information on the elk's travels in the form of GPS waypoints. To access the data, we had to recapture each elk and retrieve the collar.

It was a typical late winter day in the Nooksack River country of northwestern Washington. The morning was cool, damp, and misty, with wispy bits of fog surreally blanketing the bottomlands. The snowline was another thousand feet up on the ridge above us. The cold, moist air blowing through the openings on the right side of the helicopter, where doors usually hung, stung our faces; for darting elk, we always removed both doors on the pilot's side. Above my head, the sound of the Jet Ranger's turbine engine was a deafening roar, and I could detect the familiar pungent odor of Jet A aviation fuel combustion. I checked my rigging—a four-point harness and a tether connecting the harness to the seat frame—and adjusted my gloves and helmet. The adrenaline rush of the chase would come soon.

"Chirp, chirp, chirp…." The signal from the collar grew louder as Jess used the antenna mounted on the nose of the helicopter to hone in on this particular elk's direction and close the distance between us. "This might be tough," Jess said over the intercom as we both viewed the nearly continuous blanket of forty-year-old conifers below and around us. Darting elk in the open country of eastern Washington was generally straightforward, but this was Nooksack. Always tough. Clear-cuts were the best areas to work in these forested western Washington landscapes, but there were no clear-cuts near this elk. "Wait a second," Jess said as he sped forward and banked to our right, momentarily ignoring the direction of the collar's signal. "There," Jess said as we approached a small opening in the sea of trees—a lone gravel pit along one of the forest roads crisscrossing the area. "Not sure if she'll cooperate, but this is our only chance." Jess flew quickly back toward the signal until he was sure we'd flown past the elk. He then banked sharply, sliding behind her, and putting the elk between us and the distant gravel pit. As we got closer to her and the "chirp, chirp, chirp..." increasingly became a loud "thud, thud, thud..." in our earphones, we got our first glimpse of her as she moved gracefully through the trees below. Game on.

Patient as ever, Jess kept gently pressuring her to move in the desired direction. He did this skillfully by turning her slightly left, then right, then left, constantly redirecting her with the aircraft and keeping her line of travel toward the gravel pit. Five hundred yards, then four hundred yards, then three hundred, and two hundred. She had the advantage, and our plan was a longshot. But for now, she was doing what we wanted. We saw her on and off, flashing through tiny gaps in the forest, but the signal

The author leans out of the doorless back seat of a Jet Ranger helicopter to fire a drug-laden dart at a running elk during a field study capture on winter range near Yakima, Washington, in February 2006. | B. Berry photo.

always betrayed her location. At one hundred yards, Jess spoke over the intercom, "Heck, this might just work. Get ready." With a dart already in my rifle, I put my right foot out onto the helicopter's skid and leaned out the back seat doorway until the safety tether on my harness was taut. She was still on the line we wanted, due only to Jess's skillful maneuvering. I worked the bolt to put a live charge into the rifle's action and began to feel the effects of increasing adrenaline.

At twenty yards from the edge of the gravel pit, Jess said, "Here we go," as he closed the distance for the final hard push to get her into the gravel pit. I flicked the safety off and brought the rifle into a shooting position. She was just in front of us, slightly forward and right of Jess's door. As she broke into the open, Jess slightly dropped the collective that controlled the aircraft's lift, and we dropped almost next to her as Jess flared the helicopter and barked, "NOW!" Sensing her vulnerability on the open ground, she was running full-out—as fast as an elk can go. She was at my two o'clock position, fifteen feet below me and ten feet to my right. There was no time for precision aiming—one chance, no hesitation. I pulled the sights onto her upper left hind leg and squeezed the trigger. "Pop!" The dart flew true, and as I saw it hit her perfectly in the thigh, I shouted, "Dart in," into my helmet mic; Jess parroted, "Dart in," as he pulled back on the cyclic and up on the collective,

Helicopter darting was exciting work and a common technique for capturing elk for research conducted by the author throughout the state. | B. Berry photo.

which quickly pitched the nose up as the line of trees on the other side of the gravel pit rapidly loomed in front of us. Seconds later, the elk made cover at the tree line just before the tree line sped by below us in a blur as we cleared it. She had been in the opening for ten seconds.

Now we were back to tracking her mainly by the collar. Typically, it took seven to ten minutes for the drug to put an elk on the ground, sedated. We faced a significant challenge—the same one we always had. We needed an open space to set the aircraft on the ground (or manage a one-skid landing on a stump) fairly close to where she ended up so that I and my "mugger"—who sat to my left in the back seat—could get out and perform the necessary hands-on tasks with this elk. We needed less space than for darting, but it had to be someplace with enough clearance for the rotor blades to accommodate a safe landing—or at least touch a skid to the ground.

At about five minutes, she had stopped moving as the drug dulled her cognition. We could barely see her through the trees, and at about eight minutes she wobbled and went down. Jess took a GPS position, and then the search for a landing zone began in earnest. We were too far from the gravel pit for that to work—the roads below us were the best bet. As we backtracked on one close to her, we followed it around a corner and discovered a gap in the roadside alders that was just big enough for landing with a completely vertical descent. As the aircraft settled straight down onto its skids, we back-seaters slipped out of the open doorway with our gear and dropped to one knee next to the skids. I extended my arm to Jess's open doorway and popped my thumb up where he could easily see it—all clear. Jess made eye contact, nodded, and immediately powered up again, as he lifted straight up through our little gap in the trees.

It's not easy to find a sleeping elk in a brushy forest on foot. We knew the general direction, but we were looking for a nonreactive, prone animal in dense cover. Fortunately, we had an advantage. We'd done this hundreds of times in western Washington. Jess flew to the GPS waypoint he took where the elk had gone to sleep, used the helicopter's tracking equipment to obtain her precise location, then just hovered there above the trees. We simply had to walk toward the sound of the helicopter's roaring turbine. Well, "walk" might be understating it a bit—more like bushwhacking through blackberries, devil's club, and the like. Still, in less than ten minutes we were kneeling next to her, completing all the tasks we had to do, including retrieving the GPS collar and its treasure trove of data.

Forty minutes after darting her, I administered a reversal drug injection to awaken her from a peaceful slumber. Three minutes later, we could see consciousness return to her eyes as they rolled back into their normal position, and a minute after that she was fully alert and up on her feet again. Glancing at us in bewilderment, she quickly pivoted and disappeared back into the cloak of the forest. Mission accomplished. It was time to start all over again with a different elk.

That day in the Nooksack was typical of the field work I did throughout my career as a wildlife research biologist. In field studies of elk, deer, moose, and black bears, helicopters and small airplanes were a regular and versatile tool. I flew often—weekly at times, even daily for some projects. By my count, I flew in twelve different helicopter models and at least eight distinct kinds of small, fixed-wing aircraft during my career. I logged enough hours that, had I been a student pilot, I could have obtained licenses to fly both helicopters and small airplanes. But I was never up there to learn how to fly. I was up there to accomplish tasks like counting animals to estimate their abundance or density, finding animals with radio collars to determine their movements and survival, locating dens of radio-collared bears, or capturing animals to support various research objectives, such as we did in the Nooksack that day.

The Nooksack was the most challenging place I ever darted animals from helicopters. The terrain is steep—steep mountains dissected by deep river canyons. The forests are dense with few clear-cuts, and the clear-cuts quickly evolve into dense second-growth forest—like the area around the gravel pit. The improvised landing zones needed to reach sedated elk were hard to find and difficult to use. The weather was often problematic, especially in winter, when much of the capture work happened. We had to be creative—sometimes highly creative.

More than once, we located an elk we needed to capture in dense alder stands common in the Skagit floodplain. Two or three times, our only option was to motivate elk to swim across the Skagit River to escape the noisy aircraft, then dart the one we needed after it swam halfway across—notably, elk swim straighter than they run when fleeing a noisy helicopter—and then use the aircraft to push it into the alders on the opposite side of the river well before the drug took effect. We then landed on the shoreline rocks at the river's edge to reach the sedated elk in the alders. Jess was an exceptional pilot. He had an uncanny ability to get elk to do what we needed them to do—especially what was needed to keep them out of trouble.

Elk-capture flying was challenging and physically grueling, but it was also exciting and rewarding. We became very good at it. Even in Nooksack, we caught the elk we needed every trip. Every place where we needed to capture elk for a research project, we caught them. Most of this work was in winter. Our operations could span a week or more at a time. Getting that many days in a row of good flying weather during winter was often difficult, especially in western Washington. So, we often flew in challenging weather—we had to.

We caught elk on nice days, rainy and windy days, and in snowstorms. We always knew the limits imposed by weather and were never foolhardy—although we did things in helicopters that I'm sure would scare the pants off the average person—even on nice days. We knew the risks and thought hard about how best to mitigate them. We all wanted to go home at the end of the day. Sometimes we sat on the ground in the aircraft for hours while a snow squall burned itself out—then we flew. Other days we sat in our trucks next to the helicopter all day, waiting for a weather break that never came.

In eastern Washington we flew in brutally frigid weather with the doors off. We operated in outside air temperatures hovering around zero degrees Fahrenheit or lower—the frigid air coming through the open doorways was miserable and frosted any facial hair, including eyebrows. I wore insulated gloves—so did the pilot—but our hands were often numb, like our feet. There were days that the injectable drugs, like antibiotics or the reversals, would freeze while we were working unless we kept them inside our outerwear and flight suits, against our undergarments. I often kept darts on top of and beneath chemical heat packs so their drug contents would be liquid when I injected them into an elk. We were in and out of the helicopter, up and down steep hills, busting our way through brush thickets and brambles, breaking trails in deep snow many times a day, occasionally wrestling an elk that refused to go to sleep completely. It was physically grueling. The incessant cold also made it mentally taxing. At the end of each day, we were usually spent. But we went back the next day, ready to do it again.

We darted elk running in front of or next to the helicopter while we paced them. We darted stationary elk directly below the aircraft through a gap in a forest of thirty-foot trees. We darted elk standing thirty yards from our doors while we were in a hover by sending the dart between trees they thought they were using for cover. We darted elk crossing underneath the aircraft, running up hills, running down hills, between the skids, while flying backwards. We landed in easy, flat places—ridgetops, roads, logging landings, meadows. We also landed in difficult places—one skid on stump tops on steep hillsides where it was an eight-foot drop to the ground, on top of logging slash piles that were an obstacle course of tangled dead timber, on river gravel bars, and on steep hillsides where the pilot just touched the nose of one skid into the slope—ten percent landed, ninety percent still flying—the blade tips clearing the steep hillside by a foot. We even landed in places where someone had to jump to the ground from a skid and hand clear a place for the aircraft.

The author boards a Jet Ranger helicopter piloted by veteran wildlife capture pilot Jess Hagerman just after radio-collaring an elk for research in February 2006. A moment later, the team was in the air again, looking for another elk to capture. A full day of this work typically yielded fifteen to twenty captured elk. R. Cook photo.

Over the years, I darted at least a thousand elk. I also darted quite a few moose. Elk and moose presented distinctly different darting targets. Moose are bigger, with a more lumbering gait; they almost always move in smaller groups than elk and tend to run straight. They are larger targets and easier to dart than elk, given similar terrain. But that's where "easy" stops with moose. They are fiercely independent and confident compared to elk.

We could generally manage where an elk went after it was darted by positioning the hovering aircraft, and we could push them toward a desirable location or away from an undesirable one. If needed, we could usually change a darted elk's direction multiple times and were effective at keeping it out of trouble while the drug took effect.

With moose, we could usually turn them once—twice, if we were lucky. After that, they would typically give us something akin to a moose middle finger and stop cooperating. There were times with moose when we would try to drop the helicopter literally into their path at head level to change their direction, only to have them glare stubbornly into the aircraft as they just kept coming our way. In a game of chicken with a moose, the moose always won.

Helicopter darting was special flying—demanding and unforgiving of mistakes. The pilots were a special breed. Darting was the epitome of "living in the moment." When the chase commenced, adrenaline flowed. Focus was essential. The world as I saw it through my helmet visor grew very small. In the foreground was the barrel of my dart rifle. In the background was an elk running for all it was worth—really only a third of an elk, no more than ten or fifteen yards away, the part I would try to hit. The ground was a blur, as were trees and other landscape features that rushed past. I tried to slow things down in my mind, but it was challenging. The mugger sitting beside me in the back seat watched for hazards like wires, fences, and trees in play during the chase. I shared this duty before the chase and would return to it when the chase ended. But not this minute. The stakes were high, and we needed everyone's A game every day.

Helicopter tail rotors are vulnerable structures. Main rotor blades are stout and move at about 500 revolutions per minute (RPM). Tail rotors are light and fragile by comparison, and they turn about five times faster—around 2,500 to 3,000 RPM. Anything contacting the tail rotor, which sits much lower than the main rotor blade path, can destroy it. A tail rotor loss eliminates the counter torque necessary for controlled helicopter flight.

Lose the tail rotor and the helicopter will enter an uncontrolled spin, with the aircraft's fuselage spinning in the direction opposite that of the main rotor blades. Tail rotor loss is usually catastrophic.

Because of the critical function and fragile nature of the tail rotor, it received a lot of our attention. When we were dropping into an improvised landing zone in the field, we often had to contend with scattered trees and shrubs and uneven ground. From his front right seat, the pilot had good visibility of the main rotor path—and any threats of blade contact—in front and on each side of the aircraft. He had no view of the vulnerable tail rotor. I had to cover that and do it well or we were all in trouble. On each improvised landing, I swung my legs out onto the skids, leaned my head out, and looked back at the tail rotor as we settled into our chosen landing site. I told the pilot whether we were clear, which direction to move the tail to avoid an obstacle, or even to abort a site that wasn't going to work. We did this at least a thousand times. We never had a tail rotor contact with vegetation or the ground. But we did put the tail into some amazingly tight safe spots.

The author (yellow helmet) sits in the doorless back seat of a Jet Ranger helicopter just behind veteran wildlife capture pilot Jess Hagerman as the aircraft takes off on an elk darting operation in the Nooksack country of northwestern Washington in April 2010. These two were partners in elk and moose research captures for many years. | J. Gaydos photo.

Besides the helicopter capture work, I spent many aircraft hours radio-tracking collared animals. To radio-track with an airplane, we attached two antennas, one on each wing strut. We flew along, listening with both antennas as we scanned for collars. When we detected one, we turned while I switched back and forth between the two antennas to get the strongest signal. We kept refining the estimated direction until we could finally fly a tight circle around a tiny area with the signal always staying stronger from the antenna on the inside of the turn—the collared critter was inside that circle, even if we couldn't see it.

The ideal airplane for aerial radio tracking was one that could stay aloft for close to three hours and had high wings and wing struts for mounting the two antennas and a low stall speed (the slowest safe speed). Locating collared animals precisely required slow flight. But slow flight is also risky flight—as you approach stall speed, the safety margin declines rapidly. I tracked in several planes, but my preferred models were the Maule M-7, Citabria, Piper Super Cub, and Cessna 182. The first three were great at slow flight. Stall speeds were about forty-five miles per hour for a Super Cub and about fifty miles per hour for the Citabria and Maule. The Cessna needed more speed—no slower than about sixty miles per hour. The challenge in aerial radio-tracking is obvious—with poor landmarks below for reference, the tracker must precisely locate a collared animal by flying a circle around it while moving at near highway driving speed.

Long fixed-wing tracking flights were grueling. All the tight circling required a tolerance for positive g-force. Not everyone could do it. Airsickness usually affected more people on fixed-wing flights than on helicopter flights. Airplanes did everything faster—they had to. A helicopter's "wings" were always moving and creating lift while an airplane's stationary wings only generated lift when the plane was moving forward—fast.

Another research task for which I flew several hundred hours in helicopters involved doing aerial surveys. These were far more complicated than just flying around the countryside randomly counting animals. We used formal designs, mathematical models, and on-board technology to show where we'd been and where we needed to go. This and other technology evolved considerably in the course of my career—even the drugs we darted with changed over time. We learned many incredible things about wildlife along the way, and we learned a lot about ourselves.

The kind of flying biologists do in support of wildlife research is interesting and exciting—but also stressful and risky. Normal people don't do stuff like this. Often, our families wished we didn't do stuff like this. Helicopter captures were particularly complex efforts—managing a team of people and lots of gear; monitoring weather windows, flight plans, emergency contingency planning; and identifying staging areas and remote refueling spots. More than once, with a public roadway near an area where we would be capturing elk, we prearranged with local law enforcement or the Washington State Patrol to be prepared to stop traffic if elk headed for the roadway. We tried to think of everything that could happen—make a plan for what we wanted to happen and contingency plans in case something different happened. I rarely slept well the night before an operation. I was, after all, responsible for the welfare of my team—and the welfare of the animals we'd be chasing. I both dreaded and loved it.

Technology evolved exponentially over the course of my decades-long career. GPS collars now exist that use satellites to pinpoint an animal's location accurately and send that information to a desktop computer. A researcher can get such location information two, three times a day—even hourly, if necessary. Over half my career predated such technology. At one time, we were wowed by a simple VHF radio collar that did nothing but emit a pulsed signal. Radio-tracking animals wasn't even a widely available option until the 1960s. Unmanned drones are some of the newest innovations, and wildlife researchers are still learning how to incorporate them. It's possible that someday activities once requiring a person in an aircraft—at significant risk of harm—will be carried out using a drone flown by someone sitting in a truck or a heated office, watching a video screen.

I enjoyed the flying, mostly—the variety of missions, using so many different aircraft, and in virtually every part of Washington. I was able to see incredible things that are out of reach for most people—and I got paid to do it. I was fortunate, and I knew it. As a large mammal researcher, flying was just part of the job. Okay—an enthralling part of the job. It was usually rewarding—I saw amazing country almost every time I went up plus other critters besides the ones that were the target of my research—mountain lions, mountain goats, bighorn sheep, and a wolf. On one fall aerial survey for elk in the Mount Rainier alpine, we saw twenty bears in a two-hour flight. I witnessed more than one bull elk shed its antlers on late winter flights while I watched them from a helicopter.

We learned a great deal about wildlife that we could not have learned without being in the air. It was a unique vantage point for observing the natural world. The work promoted conservation and informed management of Washington's wildlife. We developed new, innovative tools from data we had to fly to get. I flew with a cadre of dedicated and passionate pilots I trusted deeply. Several became good friends. I also flew with many exceptional colleagues—wildlife biologists, wildlife veterinarians, wildlife enforcement officers, land managers, and technicians. We cared for each other, learned from each other, and had each other's backs—always. Much of my success is attributable to doing the work with bright, talented people who cared as much as I did about what we were doing. They earned my unwavering respect. They still have it.

It's intuitive that flying around at low altitudes in pursuit of wild animals doing their best to avoid capture is inherently dangerous. No sane biologist thinks otherwise. We believed that the chances of an accident were low if we followed our protocols—but we also knew the consequences of any flying accident could be serious. I never approached this work with a cavalier attitude. It was serious stuff. I only got in an aircraft—or asked others to get in with me—when there was a compelling reason. The objectives had to be important and, in my mind, the risks had to be manageable. I knew people had died doing this kind of work. Smart, careful, skilled people. I also read the study published in 2003 that explored the causes of on-the-job deaths of wildlife biologists. Flying accidents were the number one cause, accounting for over 60 percent of reported deaths. I had no illusions of invincibility. And I wouldn't fly with people who didn't take it deadly seriously.

Chapter 7

Tragedy

June 3, 1992—I will never forget the date nor the heartbreaking events that occurred that day. I was driving to my office midmorning, listening to my usual commuter radio program, thinking about what I needed to accomplish that day. Lost in thought, I barely noticed an interruption in the broadcast, followed by a news announcement—earlier that morning a small airplane had crashed somewhere on the Yakima Training Center, a US military facility adjacent to the towns of Yakima and Selah, where I lived. The accident had taken the lives of the private pilot and a Hanford Site biologist who worked for Battelle, my former employer. It left a second Battelle biologist critically injured; he'd been transported by a military medevac helicopter to a local hospital. My heart sank. I knew who these people had to be—they were close friends and colleagues. I felt like someone had punched me in the stomach. I could hardly breathe, and my pulse began to race.

During my time with Battelle in the 1980s, first as a graduate student and then as a staff scientist, I had two important mentors, both brilliant ecologists. Lester Eberhardt—we all called him Les—was a longtime Battelle scientist who closely guided my work as a graduate student. I learned a great deal about field research from Les, and we became good friends. My office had been right next to his, and we talked every day. Les was one of the nicest people I ever met.

Richard Fitzner—friends called him Dick—was also an ecologist, Battelle's primary ornithologist. He was a nationally recognized expert and a leader in Hanford's ecological community. Although known as a bird guy, Dick, too, was interested in my graduate elk study, but I got to know him well while living in a spare room at his house for a couple months. He was known for helping graduate students on meager research stipends. When I left Battelle in 1988, Les and Dick were leading research and monitoring of a greater sage grouse population on the Yakima Training Center—a 327,000-acre military installation—for the US Army. That work entailed, among other things, flights to radio-track sage grouse wearing tiny transmitters. In 1992, Les and Dick were using the same airplane and pilot for their project that I was using for tracking flights of radio-collared deer. The skilled Cessna 182 pilot we shared was Ray Gilkerson.

Frantic when I arrived at my office, I immediately called another colleague at Battelle and confirmed what I already knew but desperately wanted to be untrue. Les and Dick had been in the air early that morning to track sage grouse, and their aircraft went down. Dick had been in the right front seat. He was dead. The left front seat was Ray's. He was also dead—killed on impact. Les had been in the back seat. He survived the crash, but first responders found him severely injured. Army medics airlifted him to the Yakima hospital. I immediately jumped back in my car and drove the twenty miles to Yakima—never had that drive seemed so long. Running into the emergency room entrance, I saw another friend from Battelle, Lee Rogers, manager of Battelle's ecology group, at the nurse's station. Lee looked in my direction. He appeared palc, and his eyes were filled with tears as he slowly shook his head left, then right. I knew what that meant. They were all gone.

I spoke briefly with Lee, then returned to my car. Sitting there in disbelief, I felt numb. Angry. Deeply sad. Tears filled my eyes. I couldn't make sense of what had happened. It was not lost on me that just two days earlier, I had been with Ray in the same plane that now lay mangled on a Yakima Training Center hillside. I flew in that plane far more often than Les and Dick and in more unforgiving terrain. Yet, I would be with my family tonight, and they would never again be with theirs. I drove home to be alone with my grief.

The accident made no sense. It involved an expert pilot, a well-maintained aircraft, two biologists experienced with low-altitude wildlife flights, and perfect weather for flying (cloudless sky, sixty-mile visibility, virtually no wind). The crew was flying to radio-track sage grouse, but the accident site was a steep canyon that contained no sage grouse habitat, and no radio-tagged grouse were nearby. It was nearly a year before the official report of the National Transportation Safety Board investigation became available. But the events of June 3, 1992, became clear much sooner. By pure coincidence, a civilian employee working for the Training Center's environmental contractor happened to be hiking on the ridge above the accident site that morning and witnessed the tragedy unfold. That's why the accident was reported quickly and why first responders arrived in a matter of minutes instead of hours.

The canyon itself provided the key to understanding what happened that day. On a rocky outcrop halfway up the draw was a ferruginous hawk nest. This arid country hawk was declining throughout eastern Washington, and Dick was a ferruginous hawk expert. In early June there would be fledglings in the nest if the breeding pair had successfully reproduced. The witness reported seeing the plane flying up the canyon, slowing, and then—as it made a steep turn across the draw—the plane's nose dipped suddenly, a wingtip hit the hillside, and the plane cartwheeled to a stop on the slope. There was an awful sound of metal coming apart. Then the engine stopped, and there was only an eerie silence.

I can easily imagine the conversation in the plane during those last moments. Dick probably told Ray about the nest and expressed a hope that on their way to track sage grouse they could take a quick look to see if there were any fledglings in it. He may even have told Ray what amazing birds these hawks were. As they approached the outcrop that Dick probably pointed out, Ray would have slowed the airspeed, adding flaps, planning for a low-altitude pass that would give Dick and Les a good look into the nest—according to the witness, they were flying up the draw. Nearing the nest site, Ray apparently planned to bank a hard turn just above the nest—providing the two biologists with a good side window view to look for fledglings—before flying down the opposite side of the draw and then back to tracking sage grouse. Slow and low. Greater risk, but Ray had done this before. He would recover airspeed flying down the canyon on the exit. But despite Ray's experience and considerable skill, the wings' angle of attack during the turn was apparently too great for the low airspeed, and the Cessna 182 experienced a sudden and catastrophic aerodynamic stall. The wings rapidly lost lift, and as the plane dropped, one wingtip and then the nose struck the hillside as the plane began to cartwheel violently. Once the plane stalled, there was no way to avert tragedy at that altitude. The only remedy for a developing stall is to increase airspeed by pushing the nose down and diving out of it. At their low altitude, there was nothing below them but rocks and dirt.

Commonly, people who are anxious about flying fear a major mechanical failure. The engine fails. A wing falls off. Something catastrophic happens that is beyond anyone's control. In reality, only a tiny fraction of aircraft mishaps results from structural or mechanical failures. By far, the most common causes of accidents are severe weather, poor pilot judgement, or both. Ray was a good friend and an excellent pilot. I trusted him with my life regularly, just like Les and Dick. But he made a mistake. Physics would not allow the maneuver he tried that day. Approaching that unforgiving aerodynamic line courted danger. Ray knew about the line. He had skillfully flown near it before but never crossed it. For some reason, Ray's mental calculus failed that day and he crossed the line.

A professional wildlife biologist for a decade in 1992, I was aware of aircraft accidents among my peers, but those were people I didn't know. It seemed like there was an accident somewhere almost every year. But this accident took the lives of people I had relationships with and cared deeply about. People whose families I knew. People with whom I shared meals in their homes. Sadly, it was not the last aircraft mishap involving biologists or pilots I knew.

Six years after the Yakima Training Center tragedy, another Cessna 182 I flew in weekly—and whose pilot I'd switched to after Ray's accident—crashed on the Columbia River near a place called Vernita—a mere twenty miles or so from the June 3, 1992, accident site. The plane hit a static wire on a high-voltage power line over the river. The Cessna fell into the river and sank; two federal waterfowl biologists in the back seat drowned. The pilot survived, extricated himself, and swam to the surface. He was pulled into the boat of a nearby fisherman who witnessed the accident.

In 2006, a Jet Ranger I used often to capture elk and the pilot I usually flew with were in an accident during a mule deer net-gun capture in the Columbia Basin scablands. Net gunning is a technique involving a special gun outfitted with a canister holder that shoots an eight-foot-by-eight-foot net over an animal like a deer, elk, or bighorn sheep. A good friend of mine was the gunner that day. During a deer chase, a rotor blade clipped a rocky outcrop during a low-altitude turn. The aircraft was destroyed in an emergency crash landing. The pilot sustained minor injuries, but the gunner suffered a serious back injury and never net-gunned again.

A year later, tragedy struck close to home again, this time killing one of our agency's most experienced helicopter capture specialists, Rocky Spencer. Rocky was a good friend, and I had worked on captures with him several times. He had an exuberant and gregarious nature, one of the reasons he was a media darling with reporters who covered wildlife stories. To some degree, Rocky mentored all our helicopter gunners, me included. He was the best of the best.

At the time of this accident in September 2007, Rocky was net-gunning bighorn sheep in the Yakima River Canyon between Ellensburg and Selah. He loved this work and was incredibly skilled at it. Late one afternoon during the bighorn capture, Rocky exited the helicopter—an MD 500D—to handle two sheep he had just netted. The sheep were lying in a balled-up net on the opposite side of the aircraft. The helicopter was "toed-in" on a hillside with a small slope—only the front of the skids had contact with the ground. These landings were routine in this work, and this was not a difficult spot. Rocky, usually savvy around aircraft, was maneuvering around the front of the helicopter to reach the netted sheep and somehow failed to keep low enough. A main rotor blade struck his helmet, killing him. This was a devastating loss to Rocky's family and everyone who knew him.

As our department's Wildlife Program lead for aircraft safety, I was assigned to head an internal investigation and work with the Washington State Department of Labor and Industries investigator who led the external review. We all struggled to understand the accident. How did one of our most experienced people do the unthinkable? If it could happen to Rocky, it could happen to any of us doing this work. As I continued to teach aircraft safety to our biologists, and with this accident clearly in mind, I added an admonition to the classroom—the only decisions that will get you home safe tonight are the ones you make today. Having done something safely one hundred or five hundred times before is irrelevant. Only today's decisions will make a difference. Experience alone won't keep you alive.

The same year as Rocky's tragedy, Bruce Johnson, another friend working for the Oregon Department of Fish and Wildlife, was preparing to capture newborn elk calves in the Blue Mountains from an MD 500D. Just after sunrise the first day, Bruce, seated next to the pilot, was exiting the aircraft. The pilot dropped the helicopter to just above the ground; Bruce stepped down to the skid and then onto the ground in a maneuver known as a hover exit—the skids never touching the ground. The pilot, assuming Bruce was clear, lifted away. In a bizarre occurrence, the dangling intercom cord of Bruce's helmet caught on the aircraft as the pilot started to fly away, lifting him off the ground. Seconds later, the cord broke, and Bruce fell from a height of some twenty-five feet, landing in a tree. He was alive but gravely injured, with several broken bones. When rescuers reached him, they stabilized his injuries with hobbles meant for the elk calves, and he was life-flighted to a hospital. It took months of healing and therapy, but he recovered. It was a close call—nearly unbelievable. It was also a reminder of the risk wildlife biologists face in this kind of work.

In 2010, two Idaho Fish and Game biologists I knew well, Craig White and George Pauley, were darting wolves from an MD 500D when a transmission bearing failed, forcing the pilot to attempt an autorotation—a no-power, last-ditch emergency landing with free-wheeling rotor blades slowing the descent. Autorotations are effective in the open; here, there was nothing but forest below. Though the aircraft was destroyed, all three people aboard survived the hard crash landing in the trees but were seriously injured. Pilot Rick Swisher's actions were exceptional and heroic—he saved everyone's life that day.

Tragically, the list of accidents affecting people I knew professionally but not personally also grew over the years. In 2000, an MD-500 pilot and another Idaho Fish and Game biologist, a bright and fast-rising researcher named Michael Gratson, died during a mountain lion snow track survey when the aircraft's rotor struck a dead tree during a transect turn. In 2001, one of the best wildlife capture pilots in the business, John Olson, was piloting a net-gun capture of moose in Utah when he lost track of a nearby power line and backed into it while chasing a moose they intended to capture. The helicopter crashed onto a frozen lake and sank; Olson and both capture specialists in the back seat perished.

In 2009, well-known wolf biologist Gordon Haber died in a fixed-wing crash while radio-tracking wolves in Denali National Park and Preserve. More than twenty biologists have died in aircraft accidents in Alaska alone. Radio-tracking flights have also killed biologists in places like Arizona, Washington, Montana, and Minnesota. These flights often combine dangerous elements in small aircraft aviation—low and slow. Add in complicating factors—poor weather, rugged terrain, and updrafts and downdrafts in mountainous terrain—and the safety envelope becomes disturbingly small for this kind of flying. There is zero room for error. None.

In 2010, two fish biologists in Idaho and their pilot lost their lives when a loose metal clipboard flew back through the tail rotor during a landing approach, causing the aircraft to become uncontrollable and crash violently in a parking lot. That same year, all members of a Jet Ranger crew conducting an aerial survey of mule deer in California were killed when their aircraft struck a power line they had not spotted across a canyon near the survey area.

Other accidents resulted from tail booms or tail rotors hitting the ground, one from an elk running into the tail rotor during a chase. More than one helicopter crash during net-gunning operations occurred when net corner weights hit the tail rotor or main rotor. Wire strike accidents happened from time to time, and other fixed-wing aircraft stalls killed people. An industry of private helicopter vendors that specialized in large animal captures developed during the 1980s and 1990s. This was the only kind of flying they did, and they were very good at it. But their people suffered injuries or died, too. I'm not aware of any of these vendors that didn't eventually experience a serious accident.

Mitigating risk associated with flight operations is multifaceted. In the United States, Federal Aviation Administration rules require an extensive inspection and specified maintenance annually. Mechanics inspect critical systems every hundred hours on all helicopters and airplanes operating for hire—as were all the aircraft we used. Oil changes typically occur every fifty flight hours. All this care aims to ensure aircraft airworthiness. Of the accidents I tracked over the years, there was only one major spontaneous mechanical failure—the bearing failure in the Idaho MD-500 accident. Thankfully, no one died.

Pilots have a key role—obviously. I was picky about who I flew with. Having a valid pilot's license doesn't make someone suited for this kind of work. I wanted a person with a lot of flight hours and relevant experience, especially for capture work. I darted with three pilots in thirty-four years—Mel Hood, Steve Tolle, and Jess Hagerman. The right temperament was essential. Confident was good—cocky was not. I flew with more fixed-wing pilots, but even then, I only flew with ones I trusted.

The biggest risk factor in wildlife research and management flights was weather. It would be nice if biologists like me could always fly in perfect weather. Those conditions were too rare during our work seasons to make that a strict operational protocol. We tried to pick fair weather windows, but weather challenges were common.

I remember flying near Goldendale one spring while net-gunning black-tailed deer. Late in the afternoon on a day that had been mostly pleasant, we kept an eye on a distant thunderstorm cell, focused on avoiding the unpredictable winds characteristic of such air masses. Suddenly, the wind intensified even though the cell was still a mile away. We made a quick landing in a small meadow, and it soon appeared we might have to spend the night in the aircraft as the storm enveloped us. An hour later, just before dark, the wind dropped, and we were able to make a quick dash to the Goldendale airport and sleep in a motel.

Often, we would chase the better weather around an operational area—we might fly higher elevation units on days when fog blanketed lower areas and fly the lower units when the fog dissipated. We pieced together full coverage of the area over several days. It usually worked out. At times, we crept around in diffuse fog and snuck over ridgelines in misty rain.

I remember a day at Mount St. Helens when a sudden snow squall developed just after we darted an elk. We landed next to the sedated animal as the snowfall intensified. By the time we had processed her and reversed her sedation a few minutes later, the elk was covered by an inch of new snow, as was the aircraft. The squall passed after twenty minutes, and we resumed our work.

We never flew in zero visibility. That was a rule. If we didn't have visual references for the ground and any trees, we shut down. Weather was always our biggest concern—our most unrelenting source of risk. We watched weather constantly and fretted about it often. We could not control it—we just had to respond to it as best we could. It was my greatest fear.

Most wildlife management agencies have formal aviation safety programs. I helped develop ours in 2006. Recurring training, formal operational protocols, flight readiness certifications, and requirements for protective gear such as helmets and Nomex flight suits address aviation safety and mitigate risk. Mitigating risk is not the same as preventing it, but it's the best we can do short of not letting people fly.

One of the key elements nowadays in operational flight safety is a procedure known as flight following. It is not a new concept, but innovative technology has made it far more effective. Flight following is essentially what air traffic control does every day with commercial airliners. In flight following, people on the ground monitor the location and continuous operational status of an aircraft. The intent is to maintain near-real-time knowledge of an aircraft's well-being.

The premise is that, in the event of an accident or malfunction requiring an emergency landing, the crew can receive help in time to make a difference if someone instantly knows they are in trouble and knows where they are. Years ago, this was typically via regular radio check-ins, but recent technology involving an on-aircraft GPS system allows a ground-based monitor to watch the aircraft's movement across an operations area. The software sends an alert if the aircraft goes down. Indication of an aircraft that is stationary when it should be moving is a red flag that invokes a search and rescue call. Historically, lives lost on wildlife missions could have been saved had there been a rapid response and a good last-known location. Flight following might have saved them.

Wildlife flight ops are specialized applications. Uniquely useful, and uniquely dangerous. Aerial surveys, darting, net-gunning, and aerial radio-tracking all occur at low altitudes, often in difficult terrain, over water, or over natural landscapes and wild lands where places to make emergency landings—especially for airplanes—are hard to come by. At one thousand feet in the air, there is little for an aircraft to collide with apart from other aircraft. At twenty or thirty feet, there are many things—trees, power lines, cell towers, wind turbines, cable logging infrastructure, even flocks of birds spooking from the ground or a body of water.

Small airplanes and helicopters are versatile, incredibly useful tools for wildlife work. Researchers can efficiently perform tasks in the air that are exceptionally difficult—even impossible—for a person who is on foot or vehicle bound. I led studies where we had fifty or more radio-collared animals widely dispersed over a large landscape. It would have taken days, in some cases weeks, to drive around on forest roads using hand-held telemetry gear to find them all just once. We could not access animals in wilderness areas by vehicle at all. I could easily locate two-thirds of them in one three-hour radio-tracking flight in an airplane, even if half of them were deep in the wilds. But the hazards of aerial work are real. And the consequences of poor decisions or unforeseen dangers are enormous—often permanent. My wife was relieved when I no longer wore a flight suit to work. But despite the dangers, I would do it all over again. It was fascinating work, and the data we gathered made our science better.

As the years went by, I grew older and, perhaps, wiser. Admittedly, the risk weighed on me more. I also grew conflicted by the realization that I could look back so fondly on my flight experiences. They were challenging and fun days as I recalled them, but people I cared about died doing the same things. I wasn't better than them, or smarter, or more careful. I can't explain it. It could easily have been me. It could be anyone doing this kind of work. During my flying years, four aircraft I used in my work were involved in fatal accidents, and four good friends of mine died. Others I knew were seriously injured. Largely, I was lucky, even though I never felt like I was depending on luck alone. I did everything I could think of to put the odds in our favor. But I'm sure others did, too. They were bright and gifted. There was so much important work they would have gone on to do. They were genuinely good people. They were also my friends. I miss them very much.

Chapter 8

Hagerman

It was a beautiful autumn afternoon—a perfect day for flying. Even with the doors off the helicopter, I was comfortable in just my Nomex flight suit and gloves. This was way different from what Jess and I usually did when we were trying to capture elk, I thought. Much more relaxing for the moment—I could even take a nap sitting here in the back seat if I wanted. I knew that would change in just under an hour. Jess and I usually caught elk one at a time. Darting elk was anything but relaxing. Once the pursuit began, it was high-intensity, adrenaline-producing, don't-blink action. It was over fast, too. But this—this was way different.

It was October 2003. We weren't out to catch elk one at a time—we were trying to catch a bunch at once. The two-day plan was to capture as many elk as possible from the Mount St. Helens herd and relocate them to the Nooksack herd in northwestern Washington to help bolster the Nooksack's numbers. As I peered out from the back seat, I saw a second helicopter, a blue MD-500E, flying parallel to us, just as slowly. We were forty feet off the ground, fifty yards apart. Between us on the ground was a herd of twenty-five elk, slowly walking along the volcanic mudflow of the North Fork Toutle River. Our two aircraft were guiding the elk, ever so gently, toward something two miles farther down the mudflow that they had no idea existed—a special corral trap with wings—like a funnel—that extended out more than a quarter mile into the mudflow.

Darting elk involved chasing one elk at a time while it ran, panicked, for a minute or two. This was drive trapping. We were bringing elk—by the tens—to a trap some distance from where we originally found them. We did not want them running. Running that full distance would be too stressful. The plan was to walk them nearly the entire way to the trap's wings. They'd eventually figure out that something was up. Then they'd run. Hard. And that's when the real flying would start.

The two helicopters would gently nudge them toward the trap and keep them out of the forest along the edges of the mudflow. The trip to the trap would take about an hour. Easy, low-intensity flying almost all the way—and elk that were relatively calm and not exerting themselves. Confused perhaps, but not scared. We knew all of that would end in about fifty-five minutes.

We could not let them get past the trap's burlap-covered wings—each about eight feet high. Eventually we'd have to turn them into the broad end of the funnel. At first the wings would be far apart and unconfining. But we had to get them into the corral where the wings had narrowed to only fifteen feet apart. They would not like it when the two wings started encroaching on them. And that's when the real work would start. We'd get only one chance per group. Once they perceived the trap was there, they'd do everything they could to backtrack out of the wings. If they got behind the helicopters, it was game over.

We kept them moving slowly for now. The two miles became a mile, then a half mile. At a quarter mile, we could now see from our aircraft the ends of the burlap-covered wings ahead. The elk herd had no clue what was about to happen. If we could get them through the trap's open doors—emphasis on "if"—our ground crew of fifteen or so people—hidden from view for now—would close the doors behind them and drop rolled-up tarps on each wall. At least, that was the plan. As we moved them past the nearest of the two trap wings, the other helicopter slid forward on cue and passed the group, then turned slightly left across the line they'd been walking. In response, they turned slightly left, too. They were now within the ends of the funnel created by the wings. Jess and I, in the Jet Ranger, would keep them from backtracking. The two aircraft continued to make gentle, synchronized movements to keep them heading on a line and between us.

"Still looking good from here, Jess," I said into my helmet mic. Flying two helicopters near each other required both pilots to stay alert and maintain a safe distance—nothing erratic, nothing that surprised the other pilot. That was easy when we were just flying straight and parallel. We had always known that at some point keeping the elk going in the right direction would involve something different than flying straight. That's when two helicopters in the same airspace would become a problem. The elk were getting a little nervous now—each elk's movements became subtly disconnected from those around it. Heads up, ears prominently forward, their gait started to stiffen—something elk do when they perceive danger.

We were getting deeper into the wings, and the gap was narrowing. It would happen any moment now—panic. Then each elk would act in self-preservation. They would ignore herd mates and instinctively do everything possible to flee to safety. Once that happened, they would be hard to control. Our goal was to get ahead of the panic, using one aircraft to push them hard just before it all went to elk chaos.

The intercom had been quiet for a while when I heard Jess on the radio. "Tango Sierra to Sierra Bravo." These were the letters of the two aircraft tail numbers. "Sierra Bravo, go ahead Tango Sierra," came the retort from the 500E. "We are just about there, I'll call your bail-out," Jess transmitted. "Roger, Tango Sierra." The elk were now increasingly anxious—looking back and forth, mouths open and beginning to pant. A moment later we saw it, one female hit the brakes and started to pivot. Jess instantly pushed the Jet Ranger's nose down and sped forward. "We got it now Sierra Bravo—you're out." Instantly, I saw the 500E pitch up, bank hard right and disappear to our four o'clock. The airspace was all ours now. It was about to turn into a high-speed chess game. The elk would get the first move.

The straight flying was over. Now Jess would demonstrate what a Jet Ranger could do with an exceptional pilot on the stick. We closed on the group rapidly as we dropped in behind them. Dirt clods flew and decades old ash filled the air as a hundred hooves of frightened elk churned up the mudflow—they were now running hard, trying to find an out around and past us. Jess weaved and dodged, cutting them off three or four times and redirecting them toward the trap. We lost two that got behind us—*runners* we called them—but we still had most of them. Driving forward right behind the panicked elk, we could see the trap door ahead. Jess had one goal now, scare them through the gate. Make the helicopter behind them more menacing than the trap ahead.

The narrowing gap between the two wings was increasingly filled with our helicopter—banking quickly left, right, left, right. They had no place to run but forward. When they were twenty yards from the gate, Jess gave them one last hard push and flared the aircraft to a stop right behind them. We were momentarily at a forty-five-degree angle—nose up, tail down behind us—our rotor wash was now in front of us, not beneath us. They could feel it.

We were eight feet off the ground when we saw the panicked elk charging through the gate and people coming from their hiding places to slam the doors shut. A second later, the wall tarps dropped. Twenty-three elk in the trap. I felt the aircraft pitch upward as Jess pulled on the collective, and the aircraft jumped up and banked hard out of the alleyway between the wings. We—mostly Jess—had done the job. I sat in the back in amazement. Suddenly, I heard familiar voices over several of the ground crew radios. "Way to go, guys—hell of a job!" Tomorrow, these elk would be exploring their new home in the Nooksack after a four-hour trip in a fleet of horse trailers.

A spooked herd of elk is driven by helicopter down a burlap-lined alleyway toward a large drive trap on the Mount St. Helens mudflow in October 2003. In the helicopter are veteran capture pilot Jess Hagerman and the author. These elk were being captured for translocation to the Nooksack country of northwestern Washington to increase elk herd numbers there. | Scott McCorquodale photo.

I first met Jess Hagerman in the autumn of 2001. I was in my new position of statewide deer and elk research lead for the WDFW's Game Division. On that first day with Jess, I was flying as the mugger on someone else's elk research capture. By the end of that first day, my impressions were that Jess was a friendly, positive guy—and one hell of a pilot. Man, could he fly. Oh, and there was the stubby cigar—never lit, but always in his mouth.

Over the next decade and a half, Jess was my partner every time I led an elk research project anywhere in the state. I worked in partnership with others often—biologists, statisticians, wildlife veterinarians. But there was no more enduring and long-term relationship in my last fifteen years of research than the one I had with Jess Hagerman. We were together often. We were a team, and my success depended heavily on his skills. He quickly earned my respect as the best wildlife helicopter pilot in the game. I willingly put my life in his hands repeatedly. He also became a trusted friend. His is a remarkable story.

Jess was born and raised in Kellogg, Idaho. His father worked at the nearby Bunker Hill Mine and Smelter Complex. Jess and his three sisters shared a twelve-foot-by-eight-foot room with two bunk beds. The Hagerman family was of modest means but didn't lack for love, and they shared a strong family identity. You mess with a Hagerman, you mess with all the Hagermans. To make ends meet, Jess's dad regularly brought home game and fish that he harvested. On one famous occasion, he saw a beaver on a river and shot it—then stripped and swam out into the river to retrieve his protein bounty. But—it turns out—his family did not savor large rodent meat. By consensus, beaver was off the Hagerman family menu for good after that day.

Jess was a strong, gutsy kid—traits that later served him well as a pilot. He was an excellent athlete—a star half-miler in track and a talented football player at Kellogg High. After high school, Jess enrolled at Pacific Lutheran University in Tacoma, Washington. He was a football walk-on his sophomore year and made the team as both an offensive and defensive lineman—regularly playing on both sides of the ball the next two years.

When Jess returned home to Kellogg for Christmas break in 1963, he reconnected with a good friend from high school, Frank Phillips. He learned that Frank had enlisted in the United States Marine Corps (USMC) Platoon Leaders Class (PLC). The program was a path to an officer commission for enrolled college students—two six-week summer sessions at the marine base in Quantico, Virginia, and graduation secured participants a second lieutenant's commission entering active-duty basic training. The Vietnam conflict was escalating, and Frank wanted to be a part of it. He aimed to be a "ground-pounder," a leader of a USMC rifle platoon, and he wanted his good friend to share the adventure ahead.

Jess was all about adventure and challenges, and he had a keen sense of duty. After returning to Washington at the end of Christmas break, he visited a Marine Corps recruiting center in Seattle to find out more about the PLC program and what it took to be a marine infantry officer. The recruiter appreciated Jess's enthusiasm, but he reluctantly told him the Marine Corps had no current openings for infantry officers in the PLC Program. All available slots were full. Then the recruiter asked Jess a question that would change his life—"Do you think you could pass an aviation physical?" The Marine Corps had openings there.

Jess entered the PLC program as an aviation officer candidate in 1964. He became the first Pacific Lutheran University graduate to immediately enter the military under the PLC Program. On Commencement Day in 1966, he proudly wore his dress whites under his graduation gown. Immediately after being handed his teaching degree, he received his commission as a second lieutenant in the US Marine Corps. Next stop: Pensacola's Naval Air Station in Florida.

Jess's initial flight training was in the Beechcraft T-34 fixed-wing trainer, followed by the North American Aviation T-28. After successfully completing basic flight training, the pilots in Jess's class could choose between two possible tracks—tactical jets and helicopters. They all knew that whatever they flew, it was going to be in Southeast Asia, and soon. Only one pilot in Jess's class went on to fly jets—the rest became helicopter pilots. The conflict in Vietnam needed helicopter pilots—lots of them. It was one of the most dangerous jobs in the Southeast Asia theatre.

Jess immediately entered his next training phase—helicopter flight training—and he did that at Pensacola, too. His initial rotor wing training was in the TH-13M—essentially, the military version of the Bell

47—the helicopter I darted my first elk from in 1983. At Pensacola, Jess learned what aircraft he'd be flying in Vietnam: the Sikorsky UH-34—better known as the Choctaw. After finishing flight school at Pensacola, he received his United States Navy gold aviator wings—standard for Marine Corps pilots. After thirty days' leave, Jess would get a final aviation training tune-up prior to active deployment, flying the UH-34 at the Marine Corps Air Station in New River, North Carolina.

The US Army's all-purpose helicopter in Vietnam, the UH-1 Iroquois—best known as the Huey—became the enduring symbol of the American war effort. The Marine Corps flew Huey gunships, too, but they also flew Choctaws, a piston engine, bulbous-nosed aircraft with wheels instead of skids. There were a pair of main wheels in the front and a tail wheel. The Marine Corps used the Choctaw as a multipurpose aircraft, just like the army used the Huey—troop infiltration and exfiltration, medevac, supply, and fire support. The Marine Corps' Choctaws typically had a .30-caliber machine gun mounted on both sides of the aircraft, making it a formidable weapon for the leathernecks when needed.

Jess almost didn't make it to Vietnam. Given leave after finishing flight school and before his deployment, he went home to Idaho, where his dad was volunteering as a tree faller on the development of the Silver Mountain Ski Resort area near Kellogg. Jess had spent some time logging in high school, also as a faller, so he joined his dad dropping trees for the new ski runs. While Jess was lopping limbs from a fallen tree, he didn't hear the panicked warning yell from his dad, who had just dropped a tree that was falling the wrong way, right toward the unaware Jess. The tree hit Jess in the head, knocking him unconscious and giving him a serious concussion. But Hagermans are tough—and fortunately hardheaded.

Jess had one more thing to do before leaving for Vietnam. He proposed to his college sweetheart, Becky Baseler, and she agreed to marry him. I'm not sure if Becky knew the extent of the adventure she was signing on for, but they were an indomitable team from then on. Jess arrived in-country just before Christmas 1967. Having been told that most Marine Corps helicopter pilot tours were thirteen months—he expected to be home by Christmas 1968. Unfortunately, the course of the war in Vietnam changed that.

About twelve thousand military helicopters of all types flew in Vietnam in support of the United States' war effort. Nearly half were shot down by enemy fire, killing more than two thousand pilots and nearly three thousand air crewmen. This conflict has often been referred to America's "Helicopter War"—no previous conflict used helicopters and helicopter gunships so heavily for troop transport and low-level fire support. The aircraft were versatile and incredibly useful in the Southeast Asia theatre, but they were also vulnerable—they flew lower and slower than fighter jets. Being a pilot or crewman in a Vietnam War helicopter was among the most dangerous assignments for any US service member.

Marine infantrymen in a jam in the jungle or a rice paddy knew that another brave marine would be coming to help them—often flying a Choctaw helicopter and risking his own life to rescue grunts on the ground in trouble. That was the honor code for Marine Corps helicopter pilots. And Jess did more than his share of rescuing fellow marines. He remembered that he had once wanted to be where they were.

It would not take Jess long to realize what a dangerous job he now had. On one of his first missions, an enemy mortar round passed just in front of the helicopter's nose and multiple .30-caliber machine gun rounds peppered its side. After that flight, Jess turned in the standard .38-caliber revolver issued to pilots in case they were shot down and requisitioned a .45-caliber Colt M1911 semiautomatic pistol, the sidearm that ground troops carried. From then on, he flew sitting on his Colt—a weapon when needed and a mini shrapnel shield for the family jewels the rest of the time.

Jess flew Choctaw missions in some of the most well-known battles of the South Vietnam conflict. He supported the besieged First Battalion marines during the months-long Battle of Khe Sanh and flew missions during the Tet Offensive in 1968. He was shot down once, and his Choctaws took fire on many missions. Like all Marine Corps pilots, Jess displayed remarkable courage every day. He went wherever marines needed help—anyplace—any day. He earned the respect and lifelong gratitude of the grunts on the ground.

Jess finally left South Vietnam in early 1969—unbeknownst to him then, he was not done flying helicopters in Southeast Asia. Jess and Becky married soon after he returned home. They would rarely be apart again. After leaving Vietnam, Jess received an assignment as a flight instructor back in Pensacola, teaching other marines to fly the UH-34. The federal government also called on him—with other US military pilots—to fly rescue and recovery missions after Hurricane Camille in 1969, then discharged him from active duty in 1970. He made a difference in the Marine Corps. His family couldn't have been prouder.

One of Jess's last notable assignments came as a tribute to the aging UH-34s. As the Marine Corps moved to a version of the UH-1 Huey, a ceremonial flight took place at Pensacola—a formation of UH-1s and a single UH-34 flew over the base airfield. Jess Hagerman was flying the Choctaw. As the fleet of helicopters passed, Jess flew his aircraft up and away from the Hueys in a maneuver known as the missing man formation. It was the Marine Corps' farewell salute to an aircraft that had served the leathernecks well.

US Marine Corps pilot Jess Hagerman in the cockpit of a UH-34 Choctaw helicopter in Vietnam, 1968. | Courtesy Jess Hagerman.

As Jess and Becky contemplated their future, Jess was looking for a new employer, ideally involving aviation. An unexpected opportunity arose when an offer came from Air America. Prior to leaving the Marine Corps, Jess had flown to Washington, DC, hoping to fly for Air America, but nothing had come of it right away. Now, they had an offer—it would take him to Thailand and back into the right front seat of a UH-34. He went in September 1970. Becky joined him after three months. It was a secret then, but Air America was cover for the Central Intelligence Agency's ongoing effort to combat the spread of communism in Southeast Asia. The CIA connection is now well-known.

Stationed at an Air America base in Udorn, Thailand, Jess flew paramilitary missions like those he flew in Vietnam. Instead of supporting marines, he was now supporting Laos and Thailand's military forces as well as indigenous guerillas fighting the North Vietnamese Army and the Viet Cong. Most of the missions were in Laos, but occasionally the pilots flew over North Vietnam itself. Jess flew Choctaws until his last two months, when he transitioned to Hueys.

It was still hazardous flying, and the North Vietnamese surface-to-air defenses had improved, increasing the threat. United States Air Force (USAF) Douglas A-1 Skyraiders, formidable propeller-driven fighters that both the navy and air force flew throughout the Vietnam conflict, provided close air support for the Air America helicopters. These were tough, fast, well-armed planes—the last of the World War II piston engine attack planes to fly in the jet age of combat.

Air support did not equal absence of danger. One of Jess's missions took heavy ground automatic weapons fire, killing his crew chief in the back of the aircraft. Air America pilots also regularly rescued downed American aviators outside of South Vietnam who were flying missions in support of anti-communist, US objectives in the region. Rescuing downed American pilots in hostile territory was its own kind of danger.

If a pilot like Jess stayed with Air America for eighteen months, both pilot and spouse got free airfare back to the states. If the pilot stayed for three years, Air America shipped home all his belongings at no cost when his tour ended. The pay was good. It had to be—it was a dangerous job. Eventually, the Udorn operation closed down. Jess would have to relocate to Saigon if he wanted to continue with Air America, but he and Becky decided it was time to head home. They took their firstborn child, Tim, back with them. He was born in Bangkok during their Thailand stay. It was now late 1973.

Back in his home state of Washington and in need of a job, Jess updated his teaching credentials and took a position teaching history and coaching at Washington High School in Tacoma. He stayed there for five years. By now, though, flying was part of his makeup—the stick and throttle of a helicopter were like extensions of his hands—and his skills were exceptional. He missed piloting helicopters badly, and before those five years were over, he was back in a military helicopter.

In 1976, Jess joined the Washington Army National Guard as a chief warrant officer; once again he was flying the Bell UH-1 Iroquois—the venerable "Huey." He also flew a helicopter he became more familiar with later, in wildlife work. The army called the small Bell observation aircraft the OH-58 Kiowa—the civilian version was the Jet Ranger. Jess met another National Guard pilot there—Dale Ertlebrock. Dale had a full-time civilian job flying helicopters for Weyerhaeuser Aviation—the flight operations side of the Weyerhaeuser Company. The company fleet included Jet Rangers and the stretch version—Bell Long Rangers. Weyerhaeuser also had a few Bell 212s—a twin-engine civilian version of the Huey.

Dale knew Jess's passion was flying helicopters. In 1978, with Dale's recommendation, Weyerhaeuser offered Jess a pilot job. Weyerhaeuser owned and managed 2.6 million acres of forestland in Washington and Oregon. With such a big landscape, helicopters were vital to the company's operations. Jess mostly flew the Jet Rangers, and he was exceptionally good at flying Jet Rangers by now. He flew diverse missions—tree planting, spraying, tours for dignitaries, moving executives around, slash burn ignitions, water bucket hauling, photography flights, and moving gear from place to place. The company quickly designated him the Federal Aviation Administration flight examiner for West Coast Weyerhaeuser pilots. Jess was now flying full-time for his day job *and* flying for the National Guard. His logbook hours were piling up fast.

Among the lands in western Washington owned by Weyerhaeuser was a large tract of productive forestland around an ancient volcano called Mount St. Helens. The mountain was well-known in the region, but it was not a familiar name outside the Pacific Northwest on May 17, 1980. That all changed the next day.

For two months, geologists had known something ominous was happening on the northern side of Mount St. Helens. Several earthquakes, repeated steam venting episodes, and a noticeable bulge on the northern flank told scientists the volcano was awakening, but no one knew what the result of that would be. Then, at 8:32 on the morning of May 18, 1980—a Sunday—a large earthquake caused the weakened northern side of the mountain to fall away. A massive and explosive eruption quickly followed, blasting an ash cloud eighty thousand feet into the air and sending a mix of volcanic lava and rocks speeding over the landslide. At the same time, a mix of glacial ice and snowpack instantaneously melted, sending a massive and destructive mudslide westward down the North Fork Toutle River, all the way to Interstate 5.

Jess was at home that Sunday morning when he got a call from executive officers of his National Guard unit. The mountain had just erupted; the National Guard didn't know what that meant for them, but his superiors told Jess to call his section pilots and get everyone ready to mobilize in case they were needed. The pilots headed to the hangars to prep their airships for whatever was coming next. Some of the Air National Guard units were in Yakima for training.

Jess's first assignment was to fly a woman in Washington's Emergency Management Division from Chehalis to Portland. Bridges were out and she could not drive there. The National Guard instructed pilots to wear face masks—no one knew how the ash would affect people. Their superiors also warned them that the ash might shut down their aircrafts' turbine engines—airliners had developed engine trouble flying through volcanic ash before. Everyone was in uncharted territory, but lots of people were in deep trouble. The situation called for extraordinary measures—and a few heroes.

Jess flew back from Portland, landing at the Kelso-Longview Regional Airport around noon. On board was aircraft mechanic Randy Fantz. Four Air Guard Hueys were on the tarmac. A USAF Huey soon landed. Its air crew had previously moved volcanologist David Johnston around Mount St. Helens. After searching for him—unsuccessfully—they reported a vast area of complete devastation and said, in their view, no one could be alive in the area near the mountain.

Colonel Robert Watling, a Washington Army National Guard aviation officer on the ground at the Kelso-Longview Airport, was in charge of the National Guard's aircraft. Jess was intimately acquainted with the convoluted topography of the Weyerhaeuser ground near Mount St. Helens—and he knew sheltered areas might exist where injured people could still be alive. He urged Colonel Watling not to assume everyone was dead in the blast zone, Watling told him the Hueys were at his disposal. Jess decided to take two and lead them with his smaller OH-58. They headed to an area Jess knew extremely well—the South and North Forks of the Toutle River.

On the flight out, Jess was getting intel relayed from an overhead air force C-130 cargo plane doing reconnaissance. There were reports of two moving vehicles in the area where it had been assumed no one could be alive. The trio of rescue helicopters stayed the course, but soon ran into ash-filled air and increasingly poor visibility. Jess told the two Hueys to hold where they were—he and Randy would keep going a bit farther. The conditions for flying were bad and getting worse. Jess hoped his engine would keep running—so did Randy.

They began to see a massive area of blown-down timber through the ash-laden air. They got as far as Elk Rock before the visibility became so bad they couldn't continue. They turned north, then saw it—a stationary truck on the ash-covered landscape, with human tracks leading away from it. Survivors. Following the tracks, they soon found two people lying in the ash on the road. One person tried to get up, but fell back down—he tried to rise again and fell again. The other figure never moved. Jess tried to land nearby, but the ash turned into a grayout with zero visibility. He tried to see if repeated attempts to land could clear the ash from a landing zone, but it didn't work. He then flew to some nearby rocks where he toed-in with a skid and let Randy out to walk to the two victims. Jess called the two nearby Hueys in to help.

As Randy made his way, Jess tried once more to land. Dropping ever so slowly, he found the ash would clear just before the skids hit the ground if he just held steady. Straight down. He could land if he made the final descent extremely slow. The person who kept trying to get up, only to fall again, was a Russian-born logger named Jim Scymanky. Of his four-logger crew, two others had continued farther down the road, one of them leaving barefoot tracks in the still-hot ash. A Russian Catholic, the barefoot man wouldn't work on Sundays and was in the truck with his boots off when the intense heat and thick ash swept over them after the eruption. They all had ulcerated burns on their exposed faces. Scymanky appeared to have black hands—but it was not soot, as Jess first thought. His work gloves had melted and fused to his skin.

They rescued all four by helicopter, but only Scymanky survived. A few hours later, two Huey crews spotted some people walking near a campsite in the Green River valley. The Huey crews rescued them and relayed information the victims provided that a guy with a serious hip injury was somewhere nearby. Jess and Randy immediately flew in. Jess dropped Randy off to clear a landing zone on an old bridge, and they soon saw a weary, bedraggled-looking man weakly stand up in the distant brush. Jess and Randy helped him to the aircraft, flew him to the hospital in Longview, then returned and kept looking until dark. May 18 was nearly over. It had been an intense day. Some people didn't die that day because brave National Guard helicopter crews wouldn't let them.

On day two, the air search continued. Jess and the other pilots located more vehicles and searched them for survivors. There were more victims but no survivors. They took down license plates to help emergency managers contact families—they counted bodies, but they wouldn't quit searching for someone alive.

Jess got intel over the radio that a USAF Huey crew had located a family reported to be alive in the Green River valley, but another eruption prevented an immediate evacuation. When the aircraft returned, they could not find the family again. Jess and another Air Guard Kiowa quickly flew into the Green River valley to join the search and eventually spotted two adults and two children on foot near Miner's Creek. Jess landed nearby and was able to lead them to the airship. As they loaded, they tried to put a backpack into the aircraft's back seat. Jess told them there was room for people, but not backpacks. They opened the backpack to show him an infant—the backpack went in.

Visibility was poor as Jess opened the throttle and prepared to fly the family out. His Kiowa was low on fuel as the ash whipped up—visibility was now essentially nonexistent. Jess knew there was only one way out—straight up, using instruments until he could see again. As he watched the attitude indicator on the control panel during the ascent through the thick grayness, all his senses told him he was banking hard right and needed to correct by pushing the stick to the left—Jess was in the throes of vertigo. The attitude indicator showed he was level—nose to tail and left to right. Then he remembered his training—believe the ball, not what your senses are telling you—always believe the ball.

He ignored what he felt and with a steady, determined hand, continued up. Finally, at seven thousand feet, the Kiowa emerged safely from the ash into relatively clear air. Jess turned the ship toward the ground staging area and the waiting medical personnel. He looked over his shoulder at the beleaguered family—and that backpack. As the Kiowa sped west over the dense ash cloud and fuzzy glimpses of a gray landscape below that looked like the moon, he thought, maybe there is someone else who can still be saved today.

Weyerhaeuser helicopter pilot Jess Hagerman flying a company helicopter, with the snow-covered Mount St. Helens volcanic crater in the background, c. 1985. | Courtesy Jess Hagerman.

As the days passed, there were fewer miracles. The job was mostly to locate victims and document the magnitude of the tragedy that had occurred, not change outcomes. The air searches in the blast zone would at least help families know what happened to their loved ones, which was important. But the air crews that raced into the face of unprecedented dangers to save lives—and they had—they just wished there could have been more. For his valiant efforts to save civilian lives in the wake of the eruption despite the risks, Jess was awarded the Valley Forge Cross, only the ninety-fifth time the National Guard Association conferred this medal. He also received the Distinguished Flying Cross, rarely given for duty outside a combat zone.

Jess continued to fly for the National Guard and Weyerhaeuser. The corporate flight work remained diverse, but missions also began to include work for external customers. Weyerhaeuser obtained the necessary FAA certificates to operate broadly, more like commercial "for hire" flight vendors. Jess and other Weyerhaeuser pilots began to do medevac flights for the National Park Service at Mount Rainier, and they added a new kind of work—wildlife surveys and capture, mostly for WDFW. Jess and I were now on a trajectory to converge eventually—but it would be years before we met.

The landscape recovery at Mount St. Helens proceeded rapidly—first plants, then animals. Weyerhaeuser sped forest recovery by planting seedlings for the next forest. The soils were fertile—megatons of former plant and animal communities that disintegrated in the volcanic cataclysm immediately reentered the ecosystem as nutrients and chemical elements. As plants grew, elk were among the first animals to return in decent numbers. The former population died over a large area on May 18, but elk are highly mobile—perfect colonizers—and colonize they did.

No one had ever studied the complete reset of a temperate forest ecosystem following a volcanic eruption. Research opportunities abounded, and faculty at the University of Washington were particularly interested in the elk recovery that was underway by 1981. A new doctoral student named Evelyn Merrill led the field effort, and when I arrived at UW in fall 1982, Evie became my campus office mate. Before I headed to Hanford in eastern Washington later that fall to start my own graduate elk study, I went to Mount St. Helens for a few weeks to help Evie.

Weyerhaeuser helicopter pilots helped capture and radio-collar elk for Evie's study, and they also flew aerial counts. One of Jess's first wildlife flights was to take WDFW biologist Rocky Spencer around Mount St. Helens while Rocky paintballed elk in 1983. Paintballing elk from a helicopter may sound odd, and it wasn't for fun—the point of marking elk with paintballs was to develop estimates of elk numbers when it was assumable—as it always is—that many elk present in a survey area are missed during aerial surveys. We don't see them all. If biologists know how many elk have been paintballed and know how many of those elk were not seen during a subsequent survey, it's possible to extrapolate to the elk without paintballs—assuming paintballed and non-paintballed elk are missed equally.

Jess and a couple other Weyerhaeuser pilots became increasingly involved with wildlife flight ops. After paintballing with Rocky, Jess started piloting capture flights—mostly, but not only elk. Mount St. Helens was just the beginning. After Jess left Weyerhaeuser in 1992, he went to work for several private helicopter vendors—Aero-Copters, Seattle Jet, Worldwind Helicopters, and Northwest Helicopters—and he increasingly specialized in wildlife work. He loved it, had the right mental

This 2002 image captures helicopter pilot Jess Hagerman as he banks the aircraft and pitches the nose to put the darter, in this case the late WDFW biologist Rocky Spencer, in the perfect place for a successful shot at a running elk in western Washington. Note the dart, frozen in flight, nearing the elk. | Courtesy Tony Overman/*The Olympian*.

attitude and pilot's skill set, and always tried to think like the animals he was chasing. He was every bit as much a student of animal behavior as the scientists he flew with.

Jess flew often with WDFW biologists, and soon, also with the Muckleshoot Indian Tribe in western Washington. The Muckleshoots had a strong research program, and their lead biologist, David Vales, was a good friend of mine. The tribe's dependence on deer and elk for food and cultural uses was similar to the Yakama Nation's. Dave and the biologists and technicians working with him did good work in the Green River and other areas north and west of Mount Rainier.

Soon, anyone doing large mammal research in Washington—Oregon too—knew who Jess was and what he could make a helicopter do. When it came to projects where it was expected to be tough work capturing elk or deer or moose with a helicopter, conversations usually ended with someone telling the lead biologist, "I think you're going to need Jess Hagerman—he could do it—may be the only one who could." His partners expanded to include many more of Washington's tribal nations—the Point Elliott Treaty tribes, Puyallup, Lower Elwha Klallam, Quileute, Quinault, and Makah, to name a few. For a decade and a half, he was the only pilot I did this work with—that was true for Dave Vales and several others as well. He was the best I ever flew with. He was crazy good at this work—confident, focused, creative, calm, but never cocky.

Jess flew capture flights for most of the large mammals in Washington and Oregon—elk, mule deer, black-tailed deer, white-tailed deer, Roosevelt and Rocky Mountain elk, black bears, bighorn sheep, mountain goats, moose, and wolves. Once, when we were darting elk in the Nooksack of northwestern Washington, someone called his cell phone to see if he was willing to help dart polar bears in the Arctic. He piloted darting and net-gunning operations and excelled at both approaches. Jess flew Jet Rangers, Long Rangers, and MD 500s, but Jet Rangers were his go-to ride. By the mid-1990s, almost every government or tribal agency using helicopters to capture wildlife in Washington was flying with Jess. We competed for his time.

Jess has seen a lot of things. Working with Rocky Spencer one time, they were darting black bears and slinging them to a processing station where a veterinarian was surgically implanting radio transmitters. Running low on daylight one day, they decided to skip the transport bag and sling to save time—the drugged bear went into the back of the cabin next to Rocky.

About five minutes out from the processing area, Rocky told Jess that if he had a higher gear, he should use it—the bear was waking up. He was raising his head, looking around, and licking his lips when they landed. You never knew what might happen on a given day.

In 1999, Jess was flying a new Long Ranger to Canada to be repainted. Flying over Seattle, he suddenly heard and felt a loud bang, followed by extreme vibration in the controls. He had an emergency but didn't know why. He happened to be close to a helipad at the University of Washington, so he immediately plotted a descent there. He safely landed despite the aircraft continuing to vibrate badly. On the ground, he inspected the aircraft and noted some damage to the main rotor blades but had no idea what had just occurred.

Puzzling over his aircraft, Jess's cell phone rang. It was Clark Stahl, the pilot for Seattle's KIRO-7 News helicopter. Clark told Jess they just had a midair collision, and he wanted to know if Jess was okay—Clark had safely landed on the rooftop of a Seattle building. Two helicopters, running into each other over downtown Seattle—unbelievably, no one was hurt. Jess never saw the other helicopter, and he was dumbfounded by Clark's account of what had transpired just moments earlier. Clark had somehow not seen Jess until the last second and impacted his ship from behind and to the left. Clark saw Jess's tail rotor just before impact—an instant later Jess's main rotor sliced through the top of the news helicopter's plexiglass bubble, inches above Clark's head. If Jess has a guardian angel, I'm sure the dude gets overtime.

I started flying with Jess in 2001, and I darted elk with him in every part of Washington over the years. We also caught moose together. I put darts in the hind ends of about a thousand elk while leaning out of the door behind him. We caught elk where it was easy and where it was darned near impossible. We sometimes started just as the sun came up and finished at the end of the day in a landing zone illuminated by truck headlights. I often joked that my job was to shoot the dart—Jess's was to chase the elk into its path. We had a lot of success together—I wouldn't have achieved nearly as much without him. We got so comfortable together that we each had an innate sense of what the other would do in any given circumstance. We communicated over the intercom, but I grew to know what Jess was trying to do—what the shot was going to be and when he wanted me to take it.

Jess will tell you he wasn't a kid who dreamed of being a pilot. Flying was not something he thought much about, even in his teens. What led him to the pilot's seat of a helicopter was just a series of choices that presented themselves while he was trying to do something else. But if anyone was ever born to fly a helicopter, it was Jess Hagerman. He flew demanding wildlife flights into his mid-seventies—flew for over five decades and amassed more than thirty thousand flight hours in his logbooks. In aviation, that's an insane number of flight hours. I've never met anyone with anything even close, and I've been around aviation my entire career. Jess celebrated his eightieth birthday in November 2022. He served his country proudly, and his contribution to wildlife research in the Northwest is impossible to calculate. I couldn't tell my story without telling his. He is still a good friend.

Veteran wildlife capture pilot Jess Hagerman and the author with a large, sedated bull elk they had just captured in the Colockum area of central Washington in September 2013. These two partners and friends chased elk and moose across much of Washington for many years. | W. Moore photo.

Chapter 9

Elk Across Washington

As I fastened the chin strap of my aviator's helmet, I could hear the distinctive change in the turbine engine's pitch as the Jet Ranger's main rotor RPMs ramped up, followed by the familiar sensation of the aircraft getting lighter on its skids—as if it were about to start floating. Then I heard Jess ask the question over the intercom—the same one he asked before every launch when we were darting elk—"Two buckles?" I gave the expected response, as I had hundreds of times: "Two buckles!" The buckles were my seatbelt—loosely but securely fastened to allow me enough room to lean out the doorless back seat—and the locking carabiner that attached my harness to the nylon tether secured to the seat frame beneath me. I was literally strapped to the aircraft, albeit on a leash. The last thing Jess wanted was for his gunner to fall out of the helicopter while we were turning hard and fast fifteen feet above the ground to match the evasive moves of a sprinting elk. His gunner shared that perspective.

A moment later we were flying. The brisk coolness of late September air felt good on my face as it swept through the open doorway—unlike the frigid days in winter when we typically darted elk. As I looked down, the ponderosa pines thirty feet below were already passing in a green blur. We were in search mode now, intently looking for our quarry. In most of our elk studies, we focused on female elk—which told us the most about a herd's well-being. But we were starting a new project in the adjoining LT Murray and Colockum Wildlife Areas near Ellensburg, and this one was about the bulls—where did they go from season to season, what was their survival rate, and, more specifically, where were they when our winter aerial counts took place.

The elk breeding season—the rut—was nearing its peak. If we found groups of cow elk right now, we'd undoubtedly find bulls, too. We were in some good-looking country, with a mix of conifers and grassy openings where elk would likely be feeding early and late in the day. As we flew over a small draw and started up a gentle wooded slope, I heard Will Moore, sitting to my left, say, "I got elk—nine o' clock." Jess flared to slow us, then turned in the direction Will indicated. There they were—fourteen, maybe sixteen elk—moving through the open stand of pines. At the rear of the group was an adult bull, herding his harem along, working hard to keep them together—on the lookout, as always, for rivals and interlopers.

As the aircraft slid in behind and above them, I heard Jess on the intercom: "There's a decent opening at the top of this hill—that's where we're going to take them." Jess was good at this—gently moving elk where we wanted them to go in a way that made the elk think it was their idea. We watched them climb effortlessly through the trees on the gentle slope at an easy pace. They could hear the whine of the aircraft, of course, but we were well behind them by design—they were aware of us but not overly concerned. Soon, we could see the first couple elk approaching the edge of the pines at the top of the hill, and Jess began to close the gap. I moved into position with my near foot on the right skid, my upper body leaning out behind Jess's door, and I chambered the .22-caliber blank that would fire the dart from my gun. When I heard Jess say, "Get ready! Here we go," I quickly activated my hot mic so I could talk to Jess hands-free during the intense moments of the pursuit.

One by one, the group piled out of the trees into the open, breaking into a graceful trot. Only the bull was still in the forest, but he was getting close to the edge. When he finally emerged, the helicopter immediately pitched downward and descended toward him—the chase was on. I leaned against the tether and pulled the rifle stock to my cheek. As we swooped closer, Jess was careful not to overrun him—if that happened, the bull would turn off his current straight line and make things more challenging. With him out of the trees, I could now see he was a beautiful elk—big and muscular—his ivory-tipped antlers reaching to the middle of his back as he loped along. He was much larger than the cows in front of him, and he appeared to be in his prime. When we closed to about twelve feet behind him and slightly left, I pulled the trigger and saw the dart hit him square in the thigh. Jess called, "DART IN!" and the aircraft quickly lifted away. Jess kicked the tail left—nose right, spinning us so we would not lose sight of him—even for a moment—and then he started the timer on top of his control panel. Our bull was now on the clock.

At four minutes, he slowed and started to fall behind the group. At six minutes he slowed even more and began to weave left, right, left. At seven minutes he stopped and sidestepped dramatically to stay on his feet. At eight minutes he was on the ground.

Twenty minutes later, as Will and I started loading our gear back into the parked helicopter, its blades quiet and still, our bull—new GPS collar and all—trotted off in the direction of his prospective mates, intently following their scent trail. We were but a temporary distraction.

Such was the first day of radio-collaring bull elk in the Colockum country as we began a new four-year study in fall 2013. Some thirty years earlier—fall 1982—I had initiated my first-ever field research on elk. Elk had been a nearly constant feature of my career in wildlife field

A large bull elk bearing a new radio collar lies sedated after being darted from a helicopter by the author in the Colockum area of central Washington in September 2013. | Scott McCorquodale photo.

research. Although I also worked on studies of grizzly and black bears, mule deer and black-tailed deer, moose, bighorn sheep, coyotes, Canada geese, ducks, pheasants, and a few others, no species took me to the field more often or consumed more of my field time than elk.

Since 1982, I had led a large number of formal studies of elk in different Washington landscapes; designed and conducted extensive monitoring programs for several elk populations; collaborated with other scientists on their elk studies throughout the western states; regularly peer-reviewed elk research manuscripts by other biologists for several scientific journals; and received a master's degree and doctorate for my own graduate research on two different Washington elk populations.

I had also done field research on eight Washington elk herds—Rattlesnake Hills, Satus Creek, Toppenish Creek, Blue Mountains, Yakima, Colockum, Nooksack, and Mount St. Helens—and was a research partner on elk studies in the Willapa Hills as well as Mount Rainier and Olympic National Parks. I had conducted research in virtually every part

A large bull elk bearing a new radio collar awakens from sedation in the Colockum area of central Washington in September 2013. This was one of the largest bull elk the author and his air capture team darted over the years. | Scott McCorquodale photo.

of the state, often in collaboration with local biologists. Chasing the answers to an array of questions, I saw many different parts of Washington and spent a lot of field time among wild elk.

Among the most magnificent animals, elk occur in virtually every region and ecosystem of Washington. They are the most widespread large mammal in the state besides mule deer and black-tailed deer (which are subspecies of the same species). Elk densities are lowest in the shrub-steppe of the Columbia Basin, but they still live—and prosper—there. A common figure given for the statewide elk population is about sixty thousand animals, but that's more guess than real estimate. Elk are an iconic Washington wildlife species, just like bald eagles and orcas.

Two elk subspecies occur in the state: Rocky Mountain elk and Roosevelt elk. Mitochondrial DNA studies suggest there are two distinct populations of Roosevelt elk—one in southwestern Washington and one farther north, on the Olympic Peninsula. Rocky Mountain elk are widespread among several herds in central and eastern Washington, but the DNA evidence does not support confidence in more than one distinct genetic population, even though no populations share core herd areas. Roosevelt elk and Rocky Mountain elk alleles (a specific version of a gene) are broadly present in elk throughout the Cascades, suggesting either recent interbreeding or a prolonged range overlap in the far distant past. Cascades elk are clearly a hodgepodge of the two genomes. Zero elk herds in Washington are populated by only pure Roosevelt or pure Rocky Mountain elk individuals.

One of the most thrilling parts of doing wildlife field research is being physically close to our subjects—much closer than most people ever get to wild creatures. Live-capturing study animals is the epitome of this. It's an amazing experience to examine a wild animal, touch it, measure and weigh it, tag or collar it, and collect biological samples like hair or blood while kneeling next to it in the dirt. The animals I worked on—mostly large mammals—usually required sedation. Deer and bighorn sheep were exceptions, their smaller size made it possible to physically restrain them once we trapped them. Bears, elk, and moose were formidable—captures went better for us and them if we sedated them.

In all my elk research projects, we sedated elk via rifle or pistol-fired darts. They were effective tools. I enjoyed this work, but I never had a cavalier attitude toward wildlife captures. It wasn't done for fun or recreation. It was serious business. We only attempted to capture wild animals when the project objectives required it. I adopted a creed from the beginning, and people I worked with had to share that creed—whenever we made the decision to pull the trigger and send a drug-laden dart at an animal, we explicitly accepted responsibility for that animal's fate. Once under the effects of sedation drugs, they could not care for themselves. Even their ability to breathe and maintain a steady body temperature could be compromised. They were also defenseless once their cognition was impaired. We were morally accountable for the outcome. Their fate was our responsibility. If we could not live with that, we could not in good conscience attempt to sedate the animal.

We never had the opportunity to make sure the animal had been fasting, nor did we have prior bloodwork to assess risk factors or detect compromising conditions; and in the field, we lacked the advanced intervention tools you find in a veterinary clinic. There was a lot that could go wrong when sedating wild animals in a field setting, but we worked hard at being well-prepared. Wildlife veterinarians had trained us to deal with the most likely emergencies, plus we developed well-conceived protocols and obtained the best possible field-appropriate tools. We were focused on and committed to ensuring the animals' welfare. Each one we captured had inherent value as a wild creature, and that motivated us to be good at what we did. We developed a remarkable safety record—our losses were exceedingly rare. I was as proud of that as of the research results we amassed over time.

Animals in traps were simpler—they couldn't go anywhere. But in my elk research over the years, most of the elk my teams captured were darted from a helicopter. The drugs took seven to fifteen minutes to knock them down. In that amount of time, an elk can get in a lot of trouble. That was the first risk we routinely assessed—can this elk get into a hazardous situation after we dart it but before it falls over? Is there water nearby or a cliff or highway—is there dense cover they can reach before they stop moving? To some degree, we could use the aircraft to steer them away from potential trouble, and we often did that. Many times we held off darting an elk because I was uncomfortable with the risk we would have to accept in a specific setting.

Once the elk went down, the goal was to get people to it as quickly as possible. We needed to check vitals, make sure its airway was clear, and get it secured in a comfortable position for prolonged sedation. Pilots promptly dropped us off as close as possible to the drugged animal—such landing zones could be on steep hillsides, stumps, or river banks, and were often challenging for all concerned, but we wanted to minimize the amount of time a sedated animal was down before a crew member reached it to assess and ensure its well-being. We took some acceptable personal risks to minimize theirs—it was part of our moral code. We owned the outcome. Once on the ground, we hustled to our darted elk and worked quickly to accomplish our tasks and get them on their feet again.

Being close to these animals was remarkable. Kneeling next to a sleeping elk, I could smell its musky aroma. Some people might object to the odor, but to me it was a rich scent of wildness. Elk are large, muscular members of the deer family. Their amazing size and strength are even more impressive at arm's length. Their pelage of coarse outer guard hairs and dense, woollike underfur—beige torsos, dark legs, and dark mane and head—is beautiful. In the handling process—tagging, collaring, taking blood samples, giving injections to mitigate capture stress—we touched them often. It was incredible to be so close to a live, wild elk. I did my work diligently, carefully watching the chest rise and fall with each breath. These times reinforced how privileged I was to be a wildlife field researcher.

On the hoof, these animals are something to behold. When startled by people or in the presence of a predator, they move elegantly, with their noses held high and their ears forward, their trotting gait exaggerated—an alarm posture to alert other elk—it's quite beautiful. When in a full run, their loping strides can cover the length of a football field in a few seconds. They impressively and almost effortlessly jump fences, downed trees, and occasionally even elk trap walls. They wade raging rivers and are strong swimmers. As they flee danger, bulls mysteriously navigate dense timber without snagging their massive antlers on trees. Incredible.

In every elk study I led, we sought to track the movements and determine fates of individual elk for a variety of reasons. That required telemetry collars, and deploying telemetry collars required capturing elk. Marked elk facilitated meeting a host of objectives across our diverse research projects. Although we captured many elk by helicopter darting, we also used other methods. We trapped elk in panel traps, in large clover traps, by using helicopters to drive them into corral traps and processing them in livestock squeeze chutes, and we ground-darted free-ranging elk. My teams were skilled at capturing elk using whatever method seemed most likely to succeed and be safest for the animals. Our toolbox contained an array of tools, and we knew how to use them all quite well.

Sometimes my research had broad objectives. When elk permanently colonized the shrub-steppe of the Columbia Basin on the Arid Lands Ecology Reserve around 1972, it was big news. They weren't supposed to be there, according to the prevailing knowledge about elk. No one knew anything about their strategy for living year-round in a desert. My master's thesis research—described in the chapter "Twenty-seven Elk"—was a broad study of behavior and natural history of this unusual elk group. It was groundbreaking work at the time.

My elk research on the Yakama Reservation—work that supported my doctoral degree from the University of Montana—had multiple objectives. I was defining movement patterns and migration behavior, estimating survival of adult elk, quantifying seasonal habitat selection, and developing a new tool for estimating elk abundance from sample aerial counts in winter. I was working on reservation elk populations that had never been studied. Everything we learned was new information.

Other projects had more narrowly defined objectives. One of my first projects for WDFW, in the Blue Mountains from 2003 to 2006, focused on estimating survival rates and mortality sources of adult and yearling bull elk and adult cow elk. The study came about in response to a dramatic uptick in elk poaching in the area.

While leading the Blue Mountains elk research, I also led another large WDFW research project on the eastern slopes of the Cascades near Yakima. That project focused on defining cow elk movements and habitat selection and understanding the body condition dynamics of these elk, as driven by prevailing habitat conditions and their effects on elk nutrition. It was a big, complex, nearly five-year project done in partnership with the US Forest Service and elk nutrition experts John and Rachel Cook of the National Council for Air and Stream Improvement.

In 2005, we initiated a new research project in northwestern Washington—the Skagit and Nooksack River country. This elk population was smaller than most in the state and had declined substantially in the

1990s. Both tribal and state-managed elk hunting was closed down in hope of increasing elk numbers. To promote recovery, we also captured elk at Mount St. Helens and moved them to the area in fall 2003 and 2005. I was in the helicopter during those drive trap operations.

There was no rigorous approach available to estimate elk numbers in the Nooksack. No one knew how many elk there were or whether the numbers were increasing in response to actions designed to put more elk on the landscape. There had never been a solid formal estimate of Nooksack elk numbers when we started our work in 2005.

The Nooksack project focused on developing a new mathematical approach that could provide a statistically valid estimate of elk abundance. To obtain defensible population estimates, we developed a new sightability correction model and a mark-resight model application. Mark-resight models use probability estimates of resighting collared animals known to be in an area during a survey to account for both marked and unmarked animals that go unseen during aerial surveys. It was challenging, interesting, and productive work. This was a tough place to capture the study animals we needed for a successful outcome, but we caught them. It was a collaborative project. I led the work, but I worked closely with local WDFW biologists and biologists from the Point Elliott Treaty tribes. By 2007, we were generating reliable population estimates and providing evidence that the population was indeed increasing. Today, Nooksack elk are thriving and our tools are still in use.

The 1980 eruption of Mount St. Helens took me to southwestern Washington to study elk twice, twenty-seven years apart. The local cataclysm eradicated an entire generation of elk over a large swath of southwestern Washington. By 1982, elk—always great colonizers, had dispersed from a larger landscape around the blast zone to begin repopulating the range of the former elk herd. The University of Washington was studying this phenomenon. Doctoral student Evelyn Merrill, my former UW officemate, was leading the field work. Having just arrived from Montana as a new graduate student, I was ready to start my work on the shrub-steppe elk colonizers at the Hanford Site but had yet to receive my federal security clearance. Evie needed assistance, and I needed something to do for a brief time to earn my university stipend, so I was deployed to southwestern Washington to help her.

Though I was in the field at Mount St. Helens only briefly that fall, I worked on the study long enough to appreciate the incredible process that was going on with elk recolonization. In the blast zone—where the eruption had pulverized previously existing forest and animal communities and that flush of nutrients had entered the soil as incredibly rich organic fertilizer—the ground was already greening out. For more than a decade after the eruption, the landscape was fertile, productive, and a wonderful place for elk to live. Evie went on to document this in her dissertation work while I returned to Hanford to start my own work with colonizing elk.

In 2009, I returned to Mount St. Helens to lead a new elk research project under much different circumstances. Things had changed a great deal in twenty-seven years. After the eruption, much of the landscape owned by private timber companies had been replanted with young trees, and a new forest began to develop. In the first few years after the eruption, the landscape was like a huge, productive clear-cut—great habitat for elk, and they prospered. But as the forest recovered, with the help of active reforestation, the forest canopy closed, and the productive forage layer began to decline. That trajectory had big consequences for elk.

By the early 2000s, episodes of high winter elk mortality began to occur—not every year, but often. That was unusual for elk—they are typically hardy animals. There was increasing evidence that too many elk were now trying to live on this landscape. The capacity for the land to meet the needs of the elk herd (in biologist jargon, the carrying capacity) had declined and been exceeded, and elk were dying from malnutrition. As in Nooksack, no formal estimates of elk abundance existed at Mount St. Helens—not in 2009 or prior. I was assigned the familiar job of leading research to explore elk nutritional status, estimate elk survival, and develop a defensible approach to quantifying elk numbers.

There were many facets to the work we undertook in 2009. We eventually radio-collared 150 adult elk, all by helicopter darting. These elk gave us estimates of survival, pregnancy, and body fat, and those estimates formed the basis once again for deriving methods to generate formal estimates of elk abundance. I developed a new sightability correction model and a mark-resight application specific to Mount St. Helens elk.

In December 2009, a Jet Ranger helicopter piloted by veteran capture pilot Jess Hagerman sweeps in to land near a sedated elk that has just been darted by the author in the Colockum area of central Washington. The sedated elk is lying in the snow to the right of the helicopter. | W. Moore photo.

The author with a large bull elk that he had just darted from a helicopter in the mountains surrounding Mount St. Helens in February 2011. This elk, like many others, was ear-tagged and radio-collared to support ongoing research on the local elk population. The study area for this project was large, and the capture days were long. Strings of good weather days were hard to come by. | E. Holman photo.

The work lasted until 2012, and we met all our objectives. While our team was doing elk research, liberalized hunting harvests were reducing the elk density to push the elk population downward toward the new carrying capacity—unknown as it was. We developed a new population monitoring approach, as we had in Nooksack; quantified elk survival, productivity, and body fat dynamics; and gained valuable insights into drivers of winter mortality and juvenile elk survival.

Our research at Mount St. Helens was successful, but managing elk on this landscape remains challenging because direct and indirect effects of weather, plant succession, and elk density intertwine. Carrying capacity is not a fixed value—it varies in time and space. Reducing elk density should help, but there is always a time lag in the recovery of habitat under reduced herbivore grazing—an overgrazed plant community is damaged and takes time to heal. More recently, a new challenge for elk has occurred in southwestern Washington—the outbreak of a malady known as elk hoof disease. That is another story and a complex, ongoing issue.

As the work at Mount St. Helens wrapped up, I took on two new, consecutive projects on the same landscape. These were my last two extensive research efforts on elk. The study area for both was not far from home—the neighboring LT Murray and Colockum Wildlife Areas, between Ellensburg and Wenatchee. The first was a study of adult cow elk, and the second was the bull study described at the start of this chapter. Both studies focused on movement behavior, especially migration timing and the proximity of core winter and summer ranges. We also sought to obtain good survival estimates for both genders of elk.

We captured and collared 110 adult cow elk in the first study—all received GPS-equipped radio collars. During the bull project, we helicopter darted fifty-five branch-antlered bulls—all of which received GPS collars. Both were multiyear projects. The collars generated a wealth of data, and we met our study objectives. Both efforts will contribute to informed management of Colockum country elk for years to come.

By 2005, I'd been doing elk field research for over twenty years, and I thought I'd seen it all. But in late winter of that year, working on the multiyear elk study near Yakima, my crew and I had an I-didn't-see-that-coming moment. A central feature of that work was recapturing adult female elk wearing radio collars at the beginning and end of each winter. We used a portable ultrasound and additional field measurements to estimate body fat levels of these elk both going into and coming out of winter. I was collaborating with ungulate nutrition experts John and Rachel Cook from La Grande, Oregon, who had pioneered field techniques to accurately estimate the body fat of live, wild elk. We started this work in 2003, and by 2005 our process was efficient—one might even say routine. We could easily process fifteen elk in a day, even on short winter days—everyone knew their jobs and did them well.

As usual, we were rolling through our recapture list of collared elk one winter day. We'd already had a couple good days—no surprises, great data, awesome weather. I was shooting well, Jess's flying was amazing, and the crew worked like a well-oiled machine. Midmorning, we had finished handling an elk and moved on to the next one on our list. We headed to her last known location in the steep canyon country on the north side of the Wenas Valley between Selah and Ellensburg.

My receiver was tuned to our target elk, but as we crossed one canyon and then two more, we heard only the buzz of static coming through the intercom. No signal. Then, as Jess kept weaving through the terrain where we expected to find our quarry, we both heard it at the same time—the faintest "chirp, chirp, chirp…." "There! Got it!" Jess said. Pulling back on the stick, he flared the helicopter to a stationary hover, then waved the nose back and forth to get our bearing from the antenna on the aircraft's nose. "That way," Jess said as he pushed the cyclic forward again, and we sped off, tracking the strongest signal—the hunt was on. Redirecting a couple more times according to what the occasional nose wags told us, Jess was honing in, and the signal was getting stronger. I was busy prepping in the back seat for the impending shot.

As we flew over another canyon, the signal was noticeably stronger and centered on the canyon when Jess swept a ten to two o'clock arc across the canyon with the Jet Ranger's nose. "We got her now," came Jess's voice through my helmet's earphones, and off we went. As we chased the signal up the canyon, the three of us onboard were now intently scanning the rolling landscape ahead and below, looking for the dark brown heads and yellow butts of elk. The higher we flew toward the ridgetop, the gentler the wrinkled landscape became, and there were no trees. "This will be perfect," I thought. Slow pitch—middle of the plate.

Suddenly, I saw them, a small herd of about twenty-five elk loping steadily up the hillside ahead—they knew we were coming now. "Right there, Jess—two o'clock," I said. "Got 'em," was Jess's reply, "You ready?" "Ready," I replied as I leaned out the doorway with the dart gun and Jess closed the gap between us and the little group. "You see her?" Jess asked. "There, left side, fourth from the back." "Got her. Here we go," Jess said as we started the run at our target animal with its visible white collar. The grass was a blur beneath us as we caught up to and passed the last elk in the group and then the next—they were running hard now, trying to evade the noisy thing above them. With each labored breath, the warm moist exhale turned to a visible mist around each elk's muzzle in the frigid air. I could see our elk just ahead, trying to turn away from the helicopter to our right. Jess matched her moves with those of his own as he skillfully maneuvered to put her into my target zone—slightly ahead and to the right of his door.

"Almost, almost—here she comes," I thought. Then there she was, right where I wanted her for the shot. I put my sightline on her left thigh, paused, and we sped past her. We flew right through the zone where I had a perfect shot, but I didn't pull the trigger. As she disappeared behind us, Jess asked in a bewildered tone, "What do you think that was?" "Well, I'm pretty sure it was a toilet seat," I said into my helmet mic, somewhat mystified. "Yeah, that's what I thought it looked like, too," Jess responded. Both of us were at a loss for words. We realized that the signal we'd been tracking did not come from the elk I put in the crosshairs a moment ago because it did not come from a radio collar around her neck. We were in uncharted territory here.

As we circled back around on the small group, Jess asked what I wanted to do. We could just go back to tracking and find the elk we were looking for, apparently somewhere just ahead on the same line as the group we first encountered coming up the canyon. But we had all the gear needed to deploy new collars, which we did routinely. "Okay, let's get her and take that thing off," I told Jess. Immediately, without a word, he was back in chase mode as we closed on the group again. I leaned out and readied for the shot. A few minutes later, we watched our toilet seat elk stumbling along the hillside, walking a wobbly serpentine path with my dart dangling from her rear leg. She would be down soon.

As always, we had radio communication with our ground crew, which helped collect data from the elk we captured. This day, our crew included one of the agency veterinarians, Briggs Hall; John and Rachel; and one of our enforcement officers, Shawn Myers. Jess cued up the aircraft radio, "206 Charlie Hotel to Wildlife 851, you copy?" A moment later, I heard Briggs's voice reply, "851—go ahead Charlie Hotel." "Anyone got a saw in their truck?" Jess asked. I imagined the ground crew exchanging puzzled looks at this request. What would the air crew need a saw for on a treeless landscape in winter, they must have wondered collectively. Despite the mystery, Briggs told us that Shawn had a bone saw in his truck. "We're going to need it," Jess transmitted back.

By now our elk was down, in a sedated heap amid last season's dormant bunchgrasses and remnants of the winter's snow. Jess dropped my mugger and me off near the sleeping elk and flew off down the hill toward the rest of our crew. Moments later, after we had checked vitals and blindfolded our elk—we did this routinely to keep debris out of their eyes and reduce stress if their sedation level was light—we heard the Jet Ranger flying back up the canyon. Jess landed, and the crew exited with their gear—including a handsaw.

Jess had explained the situation on the flight back. There was a lot of head shaking and more than a bit of laughter as we got down to business. I cut off the toilet seat, one that looked just like mine at home, minus the elk in the middle. Rachel got busy with the ultrasound and other body measurements—she ran this part of the processing for each elk. John and Shawn put a radio collar on our elk, ear-tagged her, and gave her the usual shots to mitigate the stress of capture. A little less than an hour after Jess and I looked out our doors at something neither of us thought we'd ever see—a wild elk loping across a hill with a toilet seat bouncing up and down on her shoulders—she was awake, sporting a collar upgrade, and running off in the direction of her herd.

We surmised that at some point she had been drawn by the minerals in human urine—a known animal attractant—to an outhouse probably set up by hunters in some past season. The seat must have been up but fallen while she was nosing around for the smelly minerals. As the lid fell, she startled, ripping the toilet seat from its base, and had carried the thing awkwardly around her neck ever since. Hard to imagine any other explanation. I loaded the two pieces of toilet seat into the Jet Ranger's storage compartment—the trunk, as we called it—more souvenir than trophy. We joked that we'd probably substantially raised her social status in the herd. No longer "Old Toilet Seat Head," she now wore the best collar government money could buy. Elk bling. Never say you've seen it all.

I believe I have the honor of being the lead researcher on studies of more Washington elk populations than anyone. That's not the result of being special or gifted—I was just in the right place at the right time. The opportunities found me, and I'm forever grateful. Elk are magnificent creatures, and I still get excited each time I see one in the wild. Though researchers studied elk intensively over the last few decades, I still found questions about them that were worth chasing. And chase them I did. Those experiences were incredible, formative as a researcher, and the memories will not fade any time soon. I enjoyed the work immensely.

Of all the sounds I have heard in woods, on prairies, and over the shrub-steppe, none thrill me more than that melodic, high-pitched calliope ending with a series of guttural grunts—the screaming bugle of a bull elk in rutting season. It always stops me in my tracks and makes me more attentive. Elk are near, and that is always exciting to know. Although I still think the grizzly is my spirit animal, my extensive time in the field among scores of wild elk make them feel like kin.

Chapter 10

Buttons

People are intrigued by wild animals. Our national parks—Yellowstone, Glacier, Great Smoky Mountains, Grand Teton, Denali, Katmai, Yosemite, and the like—are swarming every summer with people hoping to see wildlife. Many have lesser known, closer-to-home places they go in hope of seeing wild birds and animals. Those seeking wildlife experiences can affect these animals, sometimes in negative ways. At times, the needs of people and wildlife conflict. For example, social media is replete with videos of predictable encounters between bison and tourists in Yellowstone—the tourist seeking the perfect selfie and the bison eventually protecting its personal space, at times to the detriment of the person with the smartphone. In wildlife management, a whole discipline has developed to deal with—prevent, mitigate, respond to—human-wildlife conflict.

Of course, wild animals sometimes impact people in human-wildlife conflicts, and that is no trivial matter. Usually, though, wild animals lose when their needs compete with ours. In many cases, it is not malevolent human intentions that result in negative impacts to wildlife. Often, people just subjugate the needs of wild animals to their own needs or desires. We rationalize that the animals' needs and ours are aligned, or perhaps complementary, or that our impact is inconsequential. Wildlife managers and biologists are sometimes called upon to navigate challenging circumstances involving people and wildlife. I became involved in one such situation a few years ago, and it affected me profoundly.

This true story of Buttons the elk is both heartwarming and tragic. She was at times a celebrity. More often she was alone in her solitary elk life. People who claimed to love her sentenced her to a life without a future—the future she was born for, at any rate. Her journey and mine eventually intersected, and we had enormous impact on each other.

The exact beginning of her story is known only to a few, and I'm not one of them. My part in Buttons's life occurred much later. She was born somewhere around 2012—in the spring, like all elk. Her mother was part of a herd somewhere near Cle Elum, Washington. As stories like this nearly always start, someone saw a small elk calf seemingly alone—possibly abandoned or perhaps orphaned. People report such concerns every year, but the young ones aren't usually orphans. Elk, deer, and moose moms often stash their babies in a hiding place while they go off to forage. It may appear there is no mother, but usually there is. Occasionally, a calf or fawn *is* orphaned, and in the case of this little elk, she may have lost her mom. It's certainly possible.

Somehow, she ended up on a rural property—perhaps a small ranch or farm. Moved by compassion, I'm sure, people decided to intervene. I don't know whether someone confined her, but she was probably bottle fed for some time. As she grew, she probably had access to alfalfa, grain, or grass hay. She grew bigger and stronger, but another thing happened, too—the distinct line most elk see between themselves and humans blurred. The instinctual fear eroded quickly. She accepted the benevolence of people, grew used to their touch and smell, and it changed her forever. But there was a cost—a high one.

As best we know, she continued to receive handouts—maybe at a livestock feed trough, a barn, or simply in a yard. Though possibly confined as a tiny calf, as she grew she was able to roam. She was free-ranging but not free. I'm sure people believed she could leave to rejoin her elk relatives anytime she wanted, but they enjoyed her visits and probably still gave her handouts. She received rewards for her intimacy with humans and became fully imprinted on them. One of them even gave her a name—calling her Buttons.

As her wanderings increased, she visited more humans and received more handouts. Those handouts were often literal—she was eating out of people's hands—people with good intentions who believed this was wonderful. Buttons became well-known among the neighbors she visited, and they looked forward to her frequent appearances. In short, Buttons became something of a community pet. They scratched her head, caressed her, took selfies with her, all the while confusing her about her identity. And always, they fed her.

The surrounding landscape was home to other—wild—elk. Certainly, Buttons could hear and smell them. Maybe she saw them at times, but they were strange, odd, scary creatures. She kept her distance, maybe even fleeing to the perceived safety of human dwellings when they were around. These elk were her kin, but that connection was only genetic by now. She felt safe only when she was alone—or better, when she was near those creatures who walked upright and fed her.

When Buttons was about four years old, she discovered another local property—Chimpanzee Sanctuary Northwest. A few miles from Cle Elum, along Highway 10, the sanctuary is a nonprofit facility dedicated to rescuing chimpanzees that have been used in medical research or privately owned as pets. The sanctuary is the permanent home of its chimpanzee residents. Diana Goodrich and J. B. Mulcahy, both chimpanzee experts, run it as codirectors. To enhance the recovery of chimpanzees and promote innate behaviors suppressed in laboratory confinement, the sanctuary includes a large outdoor enclosure with a climbing apparatus and many features to interest a wild ape.

The Chimpanzee Sanctuary must have seemed an interesting place to Buttons. She went there repeatedly. Staff at the sanctuary did not know that others had named her Buttons, but it was clear that she was habituated to people. They gave her their own tame elk name—Ellie. She seemed enchanted by the chimps that roamed and played in the outdoor enclosure. Ellie followed them along the fence line—chimp on one side, solitary elk on the other. But this place had people, too, and the elk was fond of people. Ellie got into trouble occasionally because of her attachment to humans. She tried to enter buildings where doors were left ajar, tore screens off windows, played with garden hoses and other "human" things. But the sanctuary staff enjoyed Ellie's visits as much as other locals did.

In 2016, Buttons achieved notoriety. In early July, a wildfire broke out some five miles east of Cle Elum. Fire management officials dubbed it the Hart Road Fire. Because of its proximity to homes and other dwellings, they mustered an aggressive firefighting effort. Local fire districts, fire departments from Cle Elum and Ellensburg, and fire crews of the Washington Department of Natural Resources and the US Forest Service responded. During the effort, Buttons wandered into an on-site command post where firefighters were waiting to deploy or getting some needed respite.

The crews didn't know what to think when an elk emerged from the woods, approached, and began nuzzling them—even licking their faces. It quickly became a news story, and not just locally. Outlets across the country picked up the story, including the *Washington Post*, WBBM-TV—CBS's Chicago affiliate—and Newsmax. Buttons attained celebrity status and still shunned her own kind.

It was not all good between Buttons and people. Many enjoyed her visits and her interest in humans, but some did not. Her curiosity had a mischievous element to it. She damaged property, ate ornamental shrubs, and was aggressive with neighborhood dogs. When she reached full-grown adult size, she scared some people. She didn't keep her distance. She had absolutely no fear of humans, and she approached them whether or not she knew them, including those who wished she would stay away. To some, she was a nuisance—one that could hurt somebody. She was like a five-hundred-pound puppy.

I heard about her early on, but my job then was research. Others in our agency, staff whose job it was to deal with human-wildlife issues, occasionally received complaints about Buttons. Calls came in—sometimes many—and then they stopped for weeks. Enforcement officers engaged with concerned people and gave advice. For a while, there would be a lull in the complaints, but that didn't mean that Buttons was behaving differently. There were no great options for resolving the situation, so our agency adopted a watch-and-wait strategy.

By 2019, I had a different position—I was a regional manager now, supervising biologists doing the kinds of field work I used to do. As a mentor and senior manager, I was responsible for all Wildlife Program elements in southcentral Washington—recreation, lands management, wildlife surveys, and wildlife conflicts. It was just a matter of time before Buttons drew attention again—and the next time it happened, I got the call. According to the report, she was wandering a neighborhood with a garden hose wrapped around her neck, and there was even a photo. She was in a predicament created by her affinity to people and their stuff.

Because of the risk from a hose around her neck, I advised our conflict staff to plan an intervention. We needed to sedate her and remove the hose. I also began to look more into recent events with Buttons, trying to grasp the bigger picture. What I learned was disturbing. There were still people worried about a tame, fully grown elk who believed she could go anywhere she wanted and get close to anyone who interested her.

The actions of people who saw themselves as her "friends" troubled me equally. The level of intimate contact people sought with her was alarming. She was still being hand-fed regularly—and not just hay or grain. People were feeding her cookies and, reportedly, donuts. It seemed cute to them, but it was not good for a large, wild herbivore. People were regularly petting her—even putting children on her back. There was a story of someone making a saddle for her. She had become something akin to a barnyard pony. I saw a video of her throwing a tantrum and pawing at the ground because she had not gotten as many cookies as she wanted. People obliterated the line between her and them. And they did it repeatedly, as if there were no consequences. An elk who loved people—her fans believed this was a wonderful thing.

My perspective was different. I saw elk in the wild many times. To me they were an iconic North American species, complicated in their behavior—majestic, intelligent, magnificent wild creatures. I watched them on cold mornings in a frosty meadow, their misty breath appearing with every exhale. I saw elk rutting in the shrub-steppe—several bulls screaming at each other as they bugled to lay claim to a harem of cows. An elk reduced to an object of human entertainment saddened me deeply. I knew Buttons had been born for so much more than the life people had led her to.

On the afternoon before our crew was to remove the hose from around Buttons's neck, I received a report from the field leader that she had somehow extricated herself from the hose. He asked me what I wanted him to do? By now I knew that I couldn't ignore what was happening. I'd seen too many situations where people had tamed large animals, thinking they were saving them. I could not think of a single one where the animal lived past even half of its normal lifespan. Something always happened. Sometimes the animal did something—hurt or threatened someone. An animal this large did not have to be aggressive—at over five hundred pounds, even just startling near a person could be disastrous. More often, people did something. Not all people are as benign as those who taught the animal to trust and not fear humans.

There was sure to be trouble if we just ignored her plight. We'd been lucky so far, but I knew that luck could run out any day. I conceived a plan—perhaps a last-ditch plan—surely a longshot. But we had to try. I told my staff to go ahead and get ready to dart Buttons.

Just over the hill a few miles away, our agency fed between five hundred and one thousand elk every winter in the Wenas Valley, and had been doing so for decades. The elk receive alfalfa hay every morning—from about mid-December through late February. The site is just above the fence that prevents elk from entering the Yakima Valley agricultural zone. Without the alfalfa, the elk wouldn't starve, but they'd be more inclined to go lower, and that would be a big problem. These were totally wild elk on a secluded site. They didn't roam far during the couple months we fed them. If there was any chance of rewilding Buttons, this was it. I didn't know if the plan would work. It was a Hail Mary but worth a try.

The plan was to sedate her, transport her by horse trailer to Mellotte, and release her at the Wenas Valley feed site. She would get quality food every day in proximity to wild elk who would be around for weeks and tolerated other elk well. We knew this would be a challenge for Buttons, but we hoped that, given time, her instincts would revive. As we had staff there every day during the feeding season, it was a scenario we could monitor well.

I sent a crew of my best field people. Finding Buttons was not difficult, and the darting went well on a property we had permission to use. During the capture and loading, a group of locals assembled and vociferously voiced their discontent with what we were doing. Our crew was professional and ignored the insults—they had a job to do, and they did it extremely well. We all believed we were working to give Buttons a future that did not end badly, and we tolerated some verbal abuse to achieve that goal.

The elk travelled well. When we released her at Mellotte, I got my first good look at Buttons. She was obese—easily a hundred pounds heavier than the wild elk of similar frame size had been all year. In the days that followed, we regularly heard from people who thought she'd starve at Mellotte. She was a long way from anything close to starvation. She was even a long way from a healthy weight for an elk. Misplaced human "kindness" had been killing her slowly for a long time.

People called and told me they were worried that the other elk wouldn't accept her. I said I wasn't worried about that at all. I was more worried about whether she would accept them. It was all up to her. By the next morning, when the elk came off the hill to feed, she was no longer at the feed site. She had moved into a thicket near the hay barn a few hundred yards away. She was still there the next day and the next. We monitored her closely and found she refused to have anything to do with the other elk. She could hear and smell them, but she did not identify with them.

I was transparent with the public and the media about what we were trying to do. People showed up to the gate by the hay barn and threw food over the elk fence, convinced she was starving, though she was still a hundred pounds overweight. Well-meaning folks were killing her with kindness. Saving her life hadn't stopped being a challenge.

Three days into the experiment, the feeding staff briefly left the gate by the hay barn open by accident. Thirty minutes later, we got a call from a nearby rural neighbor. They had an odd-acting elk at their porch, and it didn't move away when they went outside. Buttons was on the lam, and she went to the first house she saw. She wanted people, not other elk. I grabbed my darting gear and headed to the house in the Wenas. I hoped we would not need to sedate her again. By the time I arrived, the landowner and one of my staff had just finished coaxing her into a horse trailer. Within a couple hours of her escape, she was back by the barn on the other side of the fence. I had developed a fondness for her by this time. I never doubted that rescuing her from her original situation was the best thing for her. Some thought we were cruel, and I still got angry phone calls. But I was trying to save her life, and for weeks there was never a day that I wasn't brainstorming a solution.

Knowing that rewilding was a longshot, I had continued to work on a Plan B the entire time she was hiding by the hay barn at Mellotte. Kristin Mansfield, our wildlife veterinarian, and I were working behind the scenes on the only other option we had—permanent sanctuary somewhere. This was its own longshot. It's much easier to find permanent captivity options for less common animals—those people don't see much—grizzlies, mountain lions, wolves. A zoo somewhere will likely take a mountain lion that can't be released to the wild. But it's different for animals like deer, racoons, elk. A zoo isn't interested in a deer that people can see wild, in a field, on their way to the zoo.

We tried facilities that we had worked with before. Northwest Trek—one of our first choices—had elk and a good reputation, but they currently had more elk than they needed or could home. So, they were out. Cougar Mountain Zoo near Issaquah didn't have an elk-appropriate exhibit. Washington State University had done nutrition work with tame elk and deer, but they had no need for elk just then. Wildlife Safari near Winston, Oregon, was sympathetic. After some conversation, they agreed to take Buttons. We were elated, but the plan fell apart when the State of Oregon refused to let us bring an elk across state lines. Many states have strict rules about importing deer and elk because of concerns related to an illness called chronic wasting disease, an always fatal neurological disorder found in several states. Oregon and Washington had no known cases, but "out of an abundance of caution," Oregon would not let Buttons in.

The chimpanzee sanctuary offered to build a pen for her on their property. She could live a life of solitary confinement close to the neighborhoods where her dilemma developed and worsened. That didn't seem like the right solution. I appreciated the sanctuary staff being compassionate and wanting to help Buttons, but I wanted her to have more than just a pen.

We contacted Point Defiance Zoo in Tacoma, Oregon Zoo in Portland, zoos in Idaho, a research facility with tame elk in eastern Oregon—every place we could think of. We kept striking out and were running out of options. And Buttons was still hiding alone in the bushes near the Mellotte barn. We had one last place that had not said yes but had not said definitely no when we first approached them. It seemed like one of the biggest longshots, the world class zoo in Seattle—Woodland Park. They had an elk exhibit, which housed several elk already. They agreed to keep talking.

For about a month, I worked on Buttons's dilemma every single day—even weekends—driven to find an outcome that, if not good, was at least not bad. I continued to check on her daily. Nothing changed.

Biologists are not supposed to be sentimental about individual animals—the job is studying and managing populations. But I was determined to not fail this elk. Buttons's plight was no fault of her own. She had become what people taught her to be. A thousand acts of intended kindness had obliterated the line between her and humans and isolated her in a world where she did not fit. She was an elk, but she lived in a place that was not us and not them. Increasingly, I doubted she'd run in a meadow with other elk or ever have a calf of her own. She had a unique set of elk genes, but she was a genetic dead end—because people had decided it would be so. Were all the selfies and Facebook videos worth what people had taken from her? What was wonderful about dulling her instincts to the point where she shunned her own kind?

Buttons was one elk. Her fate would have no discernible effect on the well-being of any elk population in Washington. In the big picture, it wouldn't matter. Some people probably wondered what all the fuss was about. Why did I invest so much time and effort in this one damaged elk? I knew many would not understand. And I was fully aware from the beginning of this saga that saving her life was going to be a steep climb. I knew such stories often have a lousy ending. But I also knew that Buttons had been molded by human choices. The human stimulus was so strong that it literally overrode her basic biological instincts. She had become an island. I deeply wanted to help her out of this predicament—gain something back for her, especially a sense of her real identity. This wasn't a research problem, and it didn't have a research solution. I was not navigating it as a scientist.

I realized that because she was well-known, her story might be able to make a positive impact. This elk could possibly have a stronger voice than any agency public affairs campaign about the dangers of taming wildlife. She might be able to teach people something I could not. But that would only happen if we could save her.

While Kristin and I kept talking with Woodland Park, it became increasingly clear that Buttons was getting no closer to joining the other elk on the Wenas feed site. They seemed to terrify her. She clearly wanted no part of our strategy to give her the life of a wild elk, and we were running out of time. When winter waned, the other elk would drift away to higher elevations. It was likely she would simply stay behind—alone. I began to fear that something might happen to her while we were closing a deal with Woodland Park. To ensure we did not lose our chance to make Plan B work, we had to let go of Plan A. I told Jody Taylor, assistant manager of the Wenas Wildlife Area, and the person who ran feeding at Mellotte, that we needed to take her into our custody. He quickly prepared a suitable stall on the side of the hay barn where she'd be safe. A day later, she followed him into the stall. We were now fully responsible for her well-being, and we leaned into Plan B.

Buttons seemed content in her new location. Jody fed her daily—but alfalfa, not cookies and donuts. She still loved her human visitors—Jody, me, anybody. Our conversation with Woodland Park progressed. Some of their current elk were getting old, and they needed to plan for the next cohort. The call we were hoping for came a couple days later. There were a few hoops to negotiate, but if we could get through those, they would likely take her. The final approval on Buttons rested with their chief veterinarian—Darin Collins.

Dr. Collins required Buttons to undergo a thorough medical exam, including lab tests for an array of wildlife diseases. Many of these would be unlikely for Buttons, but zoos are careful, and we needed to make sure she had a clean bill of health. At this point, any hurdle was worth it. A few days later, Kristin arrived from Spokane, and we drove up the Wenas Valley to visit Buttons for exam day. Kristin had never met Buttons, even though we'd been working on her situation together for many weeks. Buttons greeted her warmly, nuzzling the pockets of her medical coveralls—probably frisking her for cookies. Kristin was smitten. I wasn't surprised. This was a sweet elk.

We did the initial exam while Buttons stood calmly, clueless to the fact that she was going through a physical examination. Blood draws and nasal swabs would be uncomfortable, so we eventually sedated her. She was calm enough that, while I rubbed her neck, Kristin gave her a quick hand poke with a syringe. Buttons gradually grew woozy, and we gently helped her lie down in the hay. After we finished all the sample gathering, we gave her the wake-up shot. Kristin thought this seven-year-old elk was in good health, apart from her overweight condition. The zoo could remedy that with a healthy diet.

Over the next several days, lab results came back—all negative. Several hoops cleared. We were getting closer. I felt relief—or was it joy? With all the health data in hand, Dr. Collins gave the final blessing. They would give Buttons her forever home. As with all new animals coming to Woodland Park, she would go into quarantine for thirty days, then have one last health check. After all that, she'd meet her herd mates and be free to enter the outdoor elk exhibit. I was ecstatic.

A couple days later, one of the curators and animal care staff from Woodland Park met me in Selah, and I led them up the Wenas Valley, the zoo's horse trailer in tow—plus a Woodland Park photographer. The media had been covering the saga since we took Buttons to the Wenas. Her move to Woodland Park was news, even in major markets in Seattle. Our agency had been messaging the story through the public affairs staff, and for the move, public affairs sent their lead on this story to cover the handoff to the zoo. It was an event. There would even be a Facebook live clip. Unaware, Buttons waited contentedly in her stall. She soon had new visitors, and, as always, she loved the attention.

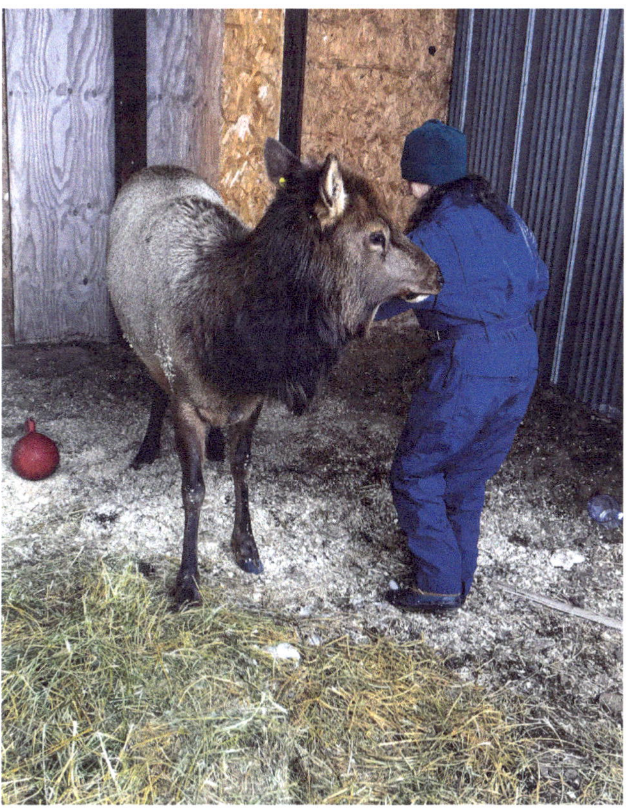

Washington Department of Fish and Wildlife veterinarian Kristin Mansfield conducts a thorough health evaluation in March 2019 of a very cooperative, strongly habituated elk nicknamed "Buttons" prior to her transfer to Seattle's Woodland Park Zoo. The story of Buttons, born in the wild but tamed by people, is a cautionary tale of best human intentions gone awry. Dr. Mansfield and the author worked closely together to prevent a tragic outcome for Buttons. | Scott McCorquodale photo.

There were interviews and a great deal of fawning over Buttons, who greeted each person enthusiastically. This was her big day, but no one was happier than me. All the work had been worth it. She would never be a wild elk. We'd tried to make that happen, but she was too damaged. From now on, she would at least live with others of her kind and receive great care at Woodland Park. She'd also see people—lots of them—every day. Her chances of living twenty years or more—possible for an elk—had increased astronomically. It wasn't a perfect outcome, but she was safe now. We had wanted to save her life, and we did. We were incredibly lucky, and I knew it.

Buttons successfully completed her quarantine. By the time the thirty days passed, the curators were already in love with her. She had that effect on people. The zoo staff had a strategy for introducing her to the other elk gradually. She had an adjustment to make. She would live with two other cow elk, Sarah and Jessie, and a vasectomized bull, Goodwyn. She couldn't go hide by a barn. She had to learn to live with other elk—but just those few. And she did.

After giving her a few days to explore the exhibit and get used to her new elk family, the zoo planned a media day to introduce her formally to the Seattle community. They invited me to attend, so I travelled to Woodland Park Zoo for the event. I intentionally arrived early to spend some time on my own, observing her in her new home before the cameras and reporters arrived. As I watched her that morning, she seemed content. Serene even. She kept her distance from the other elk but did not seem stressed as she wandered around the beautiful open-air exhibit, eating new grass shoots. I was proud of what our team and Woodland Park had accomplished on her behalf.

In permanent captivity, Buttons's world is smaller than it might have been—because people made it so. It is a cautionary tale. At its core, it is a saga driven by the dangers of habituation—a process where repeated benign experiences suppress normal instincts. Habituation often applies to a limited and specific circumstance—deer learn to ignore vehicles that pass by a field they frequent *if* the cars don't stop. In Buttons's case, it was more pervasive. She tolerated—even sought out—almost everything about people.

Habituation can occur without extinguishing the suite of natural instincts. Every day, visitors to national parks view wild animals that are tolerant of people and their vehicles—they have become accustomed to experiences without negative consequence. I have trekked with mountain gorillas in Rwanda that have habituated to visiting tourists. Even coastal brown bears in Alaska have habituated to viewing platforms from which people observe and photograph them. In these examples—animals in parks, mountain gorillas, brown bears—the animals are otherwise wild and behave like their non-habituated counterparts. They do not identify with people, and they still are wary apart from the specific context of their limited habituation. One key element lacking with Buttons—people never touched or fed these other animals. That is an inviolable rule.

When people feed animals, especially large animals, outcomes are predictably poor. The examples are many. In 2018, a crisis developed near Oysterville, Washington, created by locals feeding black bears that eventually lost all fear of people. Other residents complained when the bears became a nuisance and a perceived threat. It was a dangerous situation. When wildlife officers arrived, a bear tried to enter the cab of one officer's truck. Eventually, wildlife specialists removed ten bears. They judged five to be candidates for relocation and moved them to a distant, remote area. Five others had completely lost their fear of people. It was unsafe. Authorities ended up euthanizing the bears and donating the meat to food banks.

In Idaho in January 2022, a cow moose and her calf died in a person's yard within days of each other. These moose appeared healthy, with normal fat levels. They died from rumen acidosis—the result of people giving them unnatural, high-carbohydrate food that their stomachs could not adjust to. I've talked to frantic people who called because a mountain lion came into their rural yard and killed a deer they were feeding every day. They had created an unnatural and vulnerable situation for the deer. The mantra, "a fed bear is a dead bear" is not just about bears. The future of a wild animal that has learned to be dependent on humans for food is bleak.

Over the next few months after Buttons arrived, Woodland Park staff reported that she had adjusted nicely and now regularly interacted with the other elk. She was part of a *tiny* herd—but still, a herd of elk. Her family. Zoo staff said it was a good fit—for Buttons and for Woodland Park. She'd spend the rest of her life there. She shed her excess pounds and was much healthier. She loved the elk-appropriate snacks the curators gave her. She was also still fond of people. She bonded with her caretakers and was popular with zoo visitors. She'd finally found her place—among elk and people. It was the best we could do.

Chapter 11

The Evolution of Wildlife Research

Aldo Leopold (1887–1948), often credited as the father of modern wildlife management, was a conservationist, environmental ethicist, academic, and prolific writer. One of his greatest contributions was his articulation of the holistic concept of land as an organismal entity—the well-being of each wild creature inextricably linked to the state of the community and the land itself. Leopold's writings often heralded paradigm shifts. His widely acclaimed essay, "Thinking Like a Mountain," changed the way people understood the interplay of predators and prey and had profound effects on predator management.

Early wildlife scientists such as Leopold, Earnest Thompson Seton, half-brothers Adolph and Olaus Murie, and William T. Hornaday were extraordinary naturalists. All left a legacy principally through their keen observations, insightful interpretations of animal behavior, and their advocacy for a conservation ethos. All lived in an era before computers and advanced statistical analysis, and only the Murie brothers were still alive when James Watson and Francis Crick discovered the structure of the DNA helix in 1953.

It was a lack of relevant tools for advancing ecological knowledge about wildlife that limited brilliant minds like these and even the next generation of biologists—not a lack of ideas or an inability to think critically about what they saw. They were limited by the tools of their day. The first fully electric, digital computers weren't developed until the 1940s. The 1950s brought flexible programming languages like Fortran and COBOL; others—like C and BASIC—came even later. Practical desktop electronic calculators weren't even available until the 1960s.

When I graduated from the University of Montana with my wildlife biology bachelor's degree in 1982, no one had a personal computer. Graduate students I knew were still analyzing their data on large mainframe computers in the campus computing lab using commands fed into the computer via punch cards, not by keystrokes at a terminal—which became common practice later on. When I arrived at the University of Washington that same year, I shared an office with two other graduate students. There was no computer in that office. We received a small, shared computer a few months later, but it did only one thing—word processing. Campus computer labs were still the place where anything involving data happened, and the guts of that process was still a mainframe—they were not user-friendly.

The real breakthroughs in computer technology arrived with the development of microchips and, later, microprocessors. Both were key to miniaturization and affordability. Variants of the eventual personal computer became available in the 1970s. Many were sold as kits to mostly technology hobbyists. Computer memory continued to advance rapidly as better microchips became available, and computer graphics improved as well during that decade. In 1981, IBM released the innovative personal computer—or PC—controlled by contractor Microsoft's disk operating system, better known as "MS-DOS." A year later, *Time Magazine* dubbed the personal computer "Machine of the Year" instead of naming their usual "Person of the Year." The era of desktop computers was upon us.

The advancement of computer technology benefited all science disciplines, the study of wildlife ecology included. Mainframes and minicomputers—kind of a misnomer, because these stepchildren of mainframes were still as large as a refrigerator—were capable of complex tasks, but the learning curve to be able to direct their tasks was steep; plus they remained expensive and, therefore, not widely available. But as computers became smaller, faster, brainier, more user friendly, and less cost-prohibitive, their use by a broad array of scientists proliferated. Operating systems also became more intuitive, and discipline-specific software developed rapidly.

William Edwards Deming once famously said, "In God we trust—all others must bring data." Data is the basic currency of science. By the early 1970s, with the advent of the computer age and the development of flexible, general purpose statistical software capable of sophisticated analyses, wildlife ecologists could contemplate ever more complex questions about wild animals—if they could obtain the data. But wildlife data were difficult to acquire. As it turns out, wild animals are not that keen to be studied. Most are secretive and have an innate sense that people are a threat—even well-meaning wildlife biologists.

By the time I started my master's degree elk research on the Arid Lands Ecology Reserve in 1982, things were changing. I was able to analyze data unfettered by dependence on a mainframe computer. I still didn't have a desktop computer, but in a computer room in the next building there was a decent microcomputer. I had to share its use with other scientists, but I could perform data tasks like plotting animal observations or estimating the size and shape of elk home ranges. There were still things I did by making hand calculations with paper maps of habitat classes and roads and such. I got my first desktop computer when I began working for Battelle in 1986. It still only did simple, spreadsheet kinds of analyses. When I arrived at the Yakama Nation in 1988, my new desktop computer could do ever more complex data tasks. I was even writing code in BASIC to run analyses and create the graphs I needed. I was now riding the computer technology wave.

Many of the fundamental questions wildlife biologists have about animals—what are their movement patterns, how large are the core areas they use seasonally, what are their annual chances of survival—are best addressed by being able to follow individual animals through time—the key operative word being "follow." But following a wild animal is challenging. How do you know the deer you saw today is the same one you saw yesterday? But while computer technology was evolving, so were other technologies that would be extremely useful for those studying wildlife.

If only researchers could track wild animals at will. An obvious solution was by radio—if they could attach a radio to an animal, the signal emitted could be located via a directional antenna. The problem for decades was the radio itself. Radios that were ubiquitous in homes during World War II and in the decade following the war relied on bulky vacuum tubes—so did the transmitters that generated the signals. That made for big, heavy radios—unsuitable for even a large animal to carry. But that changed before long, and it transformed wildlife research. In 1947, engineers at Bell Laboratories in New Jersey built the first electronic transistor. By the mid-1950s, commercial transistors became available, making miniaturized radios possible—the use of handheld transistor radios exploded in the 1960s.

In 1959, twin brothers John and Frank Craighead—both wildlife biologists—undertook an incredible challenge, a field study of wild grizzly bears in Yellowstone National Park. When they proposed their study, neither had field experience with grizzlies. At the time, it was not clear how they would acquire the data they needed to answer their lengthy list of questions about these wild creatures, but they had an idea about an unproven concept.

The Craigheads were not the first biologists to ponder the possibility of hanging a transistor radio on an animal. The brothers were bright, but they weren't engineers. They knew what they wanted, just not how to accomplish it. They found help though, first from a ham radio operator they knew—Hoke Franciscus. The person key to making a functional animal radio, however, ended up being an innovative Philco-Ford electronics engineer named Joel Varney.

Varney and the Craigheads had challenges to overcome, and these were not trivial. For an animal like a grizzly to carry a functional radio, it had to be durable—a wild animal would subject a radio transmitter to considerable shock and abuse. It would also have to be impervious to the elements—moisture could not reach the internal components. A radio also requires power. In the case of an animal-borne radio, it would have to be battery power. Varney knew batteries of the day would be heavy—and the ones an animal could carry would have short lives compared to later batteries.

The VHF (very high frequency) radio band (thirty to three hundred megahertz) seemed the best choice. VHF signals propagated well outdoors, and the short wavelengths meant that receiving antennas could be small enough to be portable. Through trial and error, Varney and the Craigheads developed a workable prototype radio. They tested it short-term on a Yellowstone elk. It was still larger than they wanted. After more fine tuning, they had a hermetically sealed, durable radio that was small enough to hang on a wild grizzly—they thought. The collar's transmitter weighed but two ounces while the seven-cell battery pack weighed fourteen ounces. Some members of their team were skeptical that a grizzly bear would tolerate such a collar.

On September 22, 1961—radio collar in hand—the Craigheads found an adult female grizzly in a culvert trap they'd set the afternoon before. They first captured this bear in 1960, when she received her identifying research number—grizzly bear no. 40. They nicknamed her Marian—the name of the wife of Dick Davies, another Ford-philco engineer, and a nickname the team used often. Weighing in at three hundred pounds, she became the first Yellowstone grizzly to wear a radio. Eventually, the Craighead team collared forty-eight Yellowstone grizzlies. This changed the study of large wild animals forever.

Marian's collar worked, but Varney and the Craigheads continued to improve collar performance by tweaking the original design—introducing stronger signals and longer battery life. Tracking was still via handheld antennas or an elevated array at the research base station. But the Yellowstone team wasn't done. By 1964, they were exploring the feasibility of using external sensors paired with a radio collar to remotely transmit data such as an animal's heart rate and body temperature. This interested the Craighead team because so little was known about the denning physiology of bears.

The grizzly collars were a huge breakthrough. They led researchers to winter grizzly bear dens for the first time. They could now also study other behaviors, such as daily movements and the extent of the area each gender and age class used. They even documented social interactions of different bears wearing collars—breeding encounters of males and females or range use of females and their young from previous litters. But mountains can obstruct VHF signals, and they had a range of about one hundred miles. The Craigheads sometimes lost contact with collared bears when they entered rugged wilderness country or strayed too far. Varney wondered if they could track a collared animal by satellite. Oceanic buoys could transmit weather information to an array of meteorological satellites—why couldn't an animal collar similarly convey its location?

In 1969 and 1970, the Craigheads deployed prototype elk collars with both a VHF transmitter and a satellite transmitter—one on a penned elk at the National Bison Range in Montana and, subsequently, on two unconfined elk at the National Elk Refuge in Wyoming. The tests were successful enough to provide proof of concept. Flaws were evident—the satellite position estimates were coarse, not precise. But that got better. Within a decade, functional satellite collars became available to wildlife researchers—mostly using the Argos oceanographic and environmental satellites—well before Global Positioning System (GPS) technology existed.

It was astounding how quickly telemetry technology evolved from simple pulsing VHF transmitters that could be tracked to an animal's location—and location information was all the researcher could get—to intricate collar systems using thermistors and other technologies to encode data such as heart rate, body and skin temperature, ambient temperature, and movement rate. The frontier moved rapidly as electronic capabilities became more sophisticated—and importantly—more easily miniaturized. Transmitter systems that early on were only suitable for animals weighing hundreds of pounds or more were eventually made so small that mice and hummingbirds could wear them.

My first radiotelemetry experiences involved tracking simple VHF collars on grizzly bears in the Flathead River area with Bruce McLellan in summer 1981—handheld antennas and receivers—go find the bear. When I started my Arid Lands elk work in 1982, we purchased basic VHF collars for elk from Cedar Creek Bioelectronics Laboratory at the University of Minnesota, one of the pioneering radio-tracking labs—and vendors—at the time. For almost the next two decades, I attached hundreds of VHF collars on elk, black-tailed deer, black bears, and bighorn sheep. I spent countless hours following collared animals on foot, by truck, and from an airplane or helicopter. I wore out many pairs of boots chasing radio-collared animal locations.

An additional challenge to researchers wanting to deploy radio collars on free-ranging wildlife involved having to handle the animals. While it was possible to handle a captured, fully awake wild deer weighing a hundred pounds, an elk would be challenging—handling a wide-awake moose, bison, or grizzly bear would be foolhardy. Until the 1950s, no one had developed reliable and safe techniques for sedating free-ranging wildlife—there had been little need.

When the Craigheads arrived in Yellowstone in 1959, two challenges were on their minds—how could they track a wide-ranging animal like a grizzly through the Yellowstone wilderness, and how could they safely handle an adult grizzly to obtain weight, age, and blood, and put tags or their pipe-dream radios on them? At about the same time, British scientists in Africa were also wrestling with how to safely sedate large, dangerous wildlife.

Antonie Harthoorn, a British-trained veterinarian and early environmentalist working in Uganda, Kenya, and Tanzania, attempted to develop and refine techniques for humanely sedating free-ranging wildlife—especially Africa's large animals. Harthoorn was also the inspiration for the 1960s American television series *Daktari*. He described his amazing body of work on African wildlife immobilization in his 1970 book *The Flying Syringe*.

Harthoorn helped refine the drug delivery system—the dart gun—and he worked with colleagues such as Helmut Buechner, an American, to find better drugs for immobilizing wildlife. The Craighead and Harthoorn teams both initially started with the same drug—the primary candidate for early wildlife immobilization, succinylcholine chloride. There had not previously been a market for drugs with suitable properties for field immobilization of wild animals. Veterinarians had drugs for sedating domestic animals—relatively calm, fasting subjects that could have pre-sedation exams and bloodwork—but the wildlife context was distinctly different, calling for drugs tailored to that much less controlled environment. Without a wild animal market, no pharmaceutical company had invested in drug development for field research.

Succinylcholine was not a sedation drug at all. It immobilized animals by temporarily paralyzing them. Its effects were principally to block motor nerve impulses. Animals immobilized with succinylcholine went down—they could neither flee nor fight—but they were wide awake.

They felt fear—they felt rage—they were emotionally stressed, but the messages from their brains to run or attack went unheeded by their bodies. The paralysis also was not inherently limited to their limbs. The drug, if the dose were high enough, could also paralyze their diaphragm muscles, and if that happened, they could not breathe—they might suffocate, all the while fully awake and aware.

Interestingly, succinylcholine was—and still is—used in human medicine. Its use in humans has principally been during emergency intubations, to inhibit larynx spasms, and in electroconvulsive shock therapy, again to prevent spasmodic muscles. Different animal species have different normal levels of the enzymes that degrade succinylcholine's effects. Large herbivores characteristically have low levels and are, therefore, highly susceptible to the drug.

Early in my career, I used succinylcholine to immobilize a few elk. A dose of sixteen to twenty milligrams would routinely knock an adult elk off its feet. Elk tolerated the drug well—I never lost an elk or saw any develop breathing problems when I darted them with the drug. Bears, like people, have higher natural levels of the enzymes that reverse succinylcholine's effects. The Craigheads had to use doses of 40 to 90 milligrams to immobilize grizzlies—and they lost a few bears to overdoses.

The upsides to succinylcholine were its low cost, small dosage requirements (doses needed for large wild animals would easily fit in a small dart), quick action (it took effect in three to seven minutes), and rapid fading (animals were not down long). The downsides, though, were not trivial—it did not reduce pain perception or consciousness, there was no antidote for overdoses, and the only way to save an overdosed animal was with supplemental oxygen and artificial ventilation—difficult in the field. Many biologists believed it was not a humane way to immobilize frightened wild animals. An overdose was a gruesome death; and a terrified animal could not comprehend why it was unable to move—or worse yet, unable to breathe.

There is a famous bit of film from the 1967 National Geographic Society's documentary, *Grizzly*, that showcases the Craigheads' Yellowstone research. In the clip, John and Frank and members of their team are working on a large succinylcholine-immobilized grizzly—a bear they had nicknamed Ivan the Terrible. They are trying to tag the bear, take a plaster mold of a front paw—all the usual elements in the handling protocol. It's clear, though, that something else is happening—the bear is regaining control of his muscles. He rolls his shoulders, attempting to rise, and he's roaring as he tries to swing his head around, probably to take the arm off the closest biologist. The Craigheads keep trying to push his head back down as they tell the team to hurry with their tasks. Then, finally realizing they are out of time, the Craigheads tell everyone to run.

Ivan quickly gets to his feet, albeit clumsily. As the team dashes to safety in their vehicle, a red station wagon, the bear basically goes berserk. He trashes their equipment boxes, rams the side of the car like a mad bull, and eventually launches himself onto the vehicle's hood, raking the windshield with his six-inch claws. The last image is of the bear racing off across the meadow while the astonished voice of one of the Craigheads in the vehicle acknowledges it was a close call. When you are working on a fully awake and irritated grizzly that is only safe to be near because his limbs are paralyzed—and his limb control suddenly returns—the shortcomings of succinylcholine become obvious.

The Craighead and Harthoorn teams were both looking for something better. Both succeeded but found different solutions. In the 1960s, the bear research world discovered a new, nearly perfect drug for sedating bears. It sold under the trade name Sernylan and had great properties in wild bears—they tolerated it well, it produced full sedation and good suppression of pain perception (analgesia), there was little risk of spontaneous arousal—sudden, premature awakening—and an effective dose fit into a small dart well. Overdose deaths in bears became rare. The drugged bears I helped handle as an undergraduate near the North Fork Flathead River were all sedated with Sernylan.

Sernylan went to market in 1956. It's a drug most people have heard of by its chemical name—phencyclidine hydrochloride—better known as PCP, or angel dust. It quickly became popular among drug abusers. It had some undesirable side effects and was banned for human medicine in 1965. Its use for animals ended in 1978, and bear researchers had to find an alternative. They ended up using a common veterinary drug in the same class as phencyclidine and with comparable properties—ketamine hydrochloride. Mixed with another common drug called xylazine to prevent muscle spasms, the ketamine-xylazine mix became the drugs most carnivore researchers used in field immobilizations. It was particularly effective in bears. I personally immobilized many bears with it.

Antonie Harthoorn and his colleagues were mostly working with large African herbivores, not carnivores. Disillusioned by the negative aspects of succinylcholine, they began to explore narcotics—derivatives or analogues of morphine. Harthoorn's collaboration with others led to a new drug, a potent narcotic called etorphine hydrochloride—also known as M99. The drug was similar to morphine, but a thousand to three thousand times more potent. It was a powerful analgesic and a strong central nervous system depressant. It worked best on large herbivores when cocktailed with another drug—typically a tranquilizer like acepromazine or a sedative like xylazine. M99 was effective on everything from elephants and rhinos to small antelope.

M99's effects had a short onset, which was good in a drug for sedating free-ranging wildlife. One of the best things about M99 was that it also had a rapid reversal agent—diprenorphine hydrochloride or M5050. An animal deeply sedated by M99 would reawaken quickly after an injection of M5050. Etorphine was an expensive drug, but its biggest downside had nothing to do with how it worked in wildlife—it was deadly to people. A tiny amount would produce profound central nervous system depression and, if left untreated, death.

When I started darting elk from a helicopter in 1982 for my master's research at the Arid Lands Ecology Reserve, we were using M99, mixed with a little acepromazine. It was effective, and we used it on and off for a few years. It was not a viable choice for ground trapping elk on the Yakama Reservation with a small crew working from trucks or snowmobiles, far from medical help in case of a human exposure. Then I used the older drug xylazine—it didn't have M99's advantages, but it was safer for us to work with in a remote setting, and it was reversible.

In 1986, a newer narcotic sedative—an analogue of the drug fentanyl—rapidly became popular with large herbivore researchers. Called carfentanil, it too was deadly to people—reportedly ten thousand times more potent than morphine and four thousand times more potent than heroin. Fortunately, with all these narcotics, a good human reversal (antidote) was available—Narcan (also known as naloxone). During the 2000s, while doing elk research across Washington, we routinely used carfentanil while helicopter darting. I always had a dose of Narcan drawn up in a syringe and duct-taped to the back of the pilot's seat in front of me. Happily, I never had to use it. I was careful with carfentanil—we all were.

Tragically, carfentanil entered the common vernacular in 2002. On October 23 of that year, 40 Chechen terrorists took 850 hostages in a Moscow theatre—it was big news that day. On day four of the ensuing standoff, Russian forces wearing respirator masks stormed the theatre after dispersing a mysterious gas into the building. The Russian assault force killed all the insurgents. Sadly, more than 100 of the hostages died—some unofficial estimates put the number closer to 300—apparently after falling unconscious from inhaling the gas in the theatre. Subsequent chemical analysis of urine from one British hostage and clothing from two others identified the presence of carfentanil residue—it had been aerosolized in the gas to neutralize the Chechen rebels.

Another wildlife immobilizing drug—a drug combination packaged together—became available in the mid-1970s. Telazol combined a tranquilizer with a drug in the same class as ketamine—a drug called tiletamine. Telazol was unique in that it was safe and effective in a broad array of animals. Carfentanil worked great in animals like elk, but it would kill a mountain lion. Many of these drugs worked best—or were only safe—in a specific class of animals. Telazol was different—it was a great drug in carnivores, and it worked well in large herbivores as well. Researchers still use it widely to sedate many species of wildlife.

The Craigheads, Antonie Harthoorn, and a few others were pioneering a path in the late 1950s and early 1960s to develop humane and effective ways to capture and handle large wild animals. Finding the right drugs was just part of that. Things like dart guns evolved, too—from modified single-shot shotguns that were only modestly accurate to precision, gas-powered dart delivery platforms that look like something out of a science-fiction movie.

Biologists collaborated with veterinarians to develop standards, protocols, and training programs. Today, universities routinely have an animal care and use committee that must assess and approve any animal handling procedures for faculty and student projects. Many agencies have something similar, and most wildlife agencies today have staff wildlife veterinarians. In my time with WDFW, I routinely worked in close partnership with our wildlife vets—first Briggs Hall, and then Kristin Mansfield until I retired.

Technology marched on as well. The telemetry collar, which communicated with Argos satellites, was a landmark achievement, especially for the study of wide-ranging or migratory animals such as caribou. But that was just the beginning. In 1973, the US Department of Defense undertook an initiative that developed something called the Global Positioning System, better known as GPS. It has had profound effects on the study of wildlife. GPS became publicly available in the 1980s, but at that time, for strategic security reasons, the US military was purposefully introducing error—called "selective availability"—into civilian applications. The selective availability policy changed in 2000, which led to much more accurate GPS data in civilian systems.

Wildlife researchers needed accurate location estimates if GPS was going to help answer fundamental questions, especially about animal habitat use. So, when selective availability ended, GPS radio collars became even more attractive. The earliest and simplest GPS collars stored the location data generated on a programmed schedule in the collar itself. Researchers had to retrieve the collars to obtain the data—a system called "store on board." But the technology evolved rapidly.

Today, GPS collars are far more advanced. Instead of needing to retrieve a collar to obtain the GPS fix data, it can be uplinked to satellite phone orbiters and the data then retransmitted to a desktop computer via a collar vendor's server. Researchers can accumulate several locations of their study animals in a day and never leave their office—though I recommend they find other reasons to get their boots dirty. It is even possible now to have two-way communication with GPS collars, allowing for remote reprogramming—for example, to obtain fixes on a different schedule of specific times.

In 2003, I attached my first GPS collars on elk. They were clunky, temperamental, and expensive. They struggled when the collared animal was under a forest canopy. But I could now get data on where the animals had been on days when I was not in the field pursuing them. By 2013, I was putting GPS collars on bull elk in the LT Murray and Colockum Wildlife Areas that would send data to my computer multiple times a day, and these worked well in stands of trees. I was getting an order of magnitude more data, but I missed the intimacy of tracking an animal through the woods with an antenna in my hand to find where it was that day.

Wildlife biologists are fundamentally trying to answer questions and test hypotheses about wildlife as a means of advancing conservation and intelligent management. Tools that promote collection of field data are important—exceptionally so. But another area of considerable evolution has been what researchers can do with that data. University programs for aspiring biologists include more than just courses about wildlife—botany, forestry and range management, technical writing, chemistry, geography, ecology (not just animals), plus math and statistics are common coursework. That was the case even when I entered college in 1979.

Naturalists are interpreters of experience—what they can see, hear, or touch. Insights based on critical thinking and extensive time afield have enormous value, especially if the observer is also a good communicator. At one time, wildlife biologists were mostly naturalists—the passion of a naturalist still lives in the belly of most wildlife scientists. I know it does in me. But it was inevitable that wildlife biologists would wrestle with questions they could not answer simply by being critical observers or using only a calculator and a pad of paper. All the sciences have become more quantitative with time—wildlife biology included. As computer technology became more sophisticated and accessible, bright minds wanted more from data. A naturalist's observations may lead them to conclude that there are a lot of deer—or not many. The question of actual deer numbers is not easily answered. The science of wildlife biology has grown increasingly quantitative—to be relevant, it had to.

Talking about statistics will make most nonscientists' eyes glaze over. It may also ensure you don't get invited to the next dinner party. So, suffice to say that some brilliant biometricians (statisticians of biological data) and gifted quantitative biologists have, with time, bequeathed the science of wildlife with incredible tools for analyzing data—people like

George Seber, George Jolly, Emily Schnabel, Gary White, Ken Burnham, Ken Pollock, Andy Royle, Lee Eberhardt, David Anderson, Bryan Manly, Jeff Laake, and Steve Buckland, to name just a few.

In particular, such contributors developed methods and software to estimate things that have no closed form solution—for example, 2 + 2 = 4 is a closed form solution yielding a finite answer that is easily calculated and always the same. Many unknowns that biologists want good estimates for, like density or survival, can only be derived in the context of probability—the probability that the real unknown value is more or less likely to be a specific number, based on the data in hand. Many questions about wildlife are complex and nearly intractable, but over many decades, better and increasingly sophisticated tools to analyze data were created. This is not a trivial aspect of wildlife research evolution.

Another technological and analytic advancement that evolved dramatically over the course of my career was hardware and software that collectively became known as geographic information systems (GIS). Many of the questions biologists pursue have their roots in the relationship between animals and the environments they live in. Where are specific habitats they use; what are elevations, slopes, and aspects of the terrain traversed by study animals; how far from roads or water are telemetry datapoints? Early on, biologists used maps and mylar overlays with hand-drawn polygons, rulers, and calculators to clumsily derive such data. But maps eventually became digitized, and each pixel on a map could have associated data—cover type, forest stand age, distance to the nearest road or stream, slope, aspect, and much more.

By the 1960s, some bright people, notably Roger Tomlinson, a Canadian, foresaw the concept of broadly useful digital environmental data—information-rich maps on computers. Tomlinson derived the first functional and practical GIS—the Canada Geographic Information System. It initially supported an effort known as the Canada Land Inventory, but it was never in the public domain. Tomlinson's work was proof of concept, and other contributors advanced the GIS model and made it universally available. Harvard University's Laboratory for Computer Graphics and Spatial Analysis generated significant software elements that took seminal steps forward in the evolution of GIS and provided easy access to an array of research entities. By the late 1970s, two public domain GIS packages—Map Overlay and Statistical System (MOSS) and Geographic Resources Analysis Support System (GRASS)—were developed and subsequently released. I used GRASS briefly in the late 1980s—my first personal experience with GIS.

GIS technology has rapidly and continually evolved since the 1970s. There are now many applications and many vendor-specific packages. There are even desktop GIS packages now. Two prominent entities emerged as major GIS developers—Earth Resource Data Analysis System (ERDAS) and Environmental Systems Research Institute (ESRI). The ESRI GIS environment ArcGIS dominates the market for GIS software used in ecological research. I've used it many times in my work. There are no researchers today who do not rely heavily on GIS data and analyses when exploring questions such as wildlife habitat selection or environmental modeling of animal behavior such as movements. The integration of remotely-sensed data—from aircraft or satellites—and GIS technology has become an incredibly useful and powerful tool. As an associate editor of a research journal from 2003 until my retirement, it was exceedingly rare for me to review manuscripts that did not employ GIS in some way.

The rapid and ongoing development of DNA technology and applications profoundly affected nearly every scientific discipline. These advancements have transformed wildlife biology, too. Some applications are obvious—are two or more populations of animals related—are they genetically isolated or is gene flow evident? Are subspecies designations defensible? Is a population inbred or still genetically diverse? What source population is best suited for reintroduction to a former range of a species?

Over the last few decades, DNA applications have become broader and more commonly used in wildlife biology. A whole quantitative realm had already developed to approach estimating density or population size from methods known as mark-recapture. Initially, these techniques—dependent on estimating detection rates from encounter histories of marked animals—relied on animals with physical marks placed on them by biologists (tags or tattoos, for example). If we could estimate the probability of detecting a specific individual from how often it was recaptured under some multiple survey protocol, the detection probability could be applied to all animals captured, even ones that had never been seen before in any given survey.

DNA techniques offered a whole new possibility—the detection of known individuals that no human hand had ever touched or no human eye had seen. Hair or digestive tract cells in feces could yield DNA profiles specific to an individual animal. This was an absolute game changer. Biologists could now entice an animal like a bear to a smelly bait site where a piece of barbed wire was set to snag a few hairs. Those hairs could be analyzed with DNA methods to create a tally of known individuals. A second similar survey would yield hairs with DNA signatures matching some bears from the first survey plus hairs from bears that had not been sampled the first time around. There was no need to catch a large sample of bears and tag them to create a means of estimating detection rates. Individual DNA profiles can yield the same information without ever having to catch and mark a single bear. This is now a common approach in the field of mark-recapture.

The challenge with such methods is often the collection of the actual DNA samples, especially for secretive, low-density animals (wolverines, jaguars, snow leopards, and such). Bears are easy, but not all wildlife species are. What if there was a way to do more than passively wait for the samples? What if you could actively pursue those samples? Some bright people wondered if dogs, with their keen sense of smell, could help. In fact, they can, and they are good at it.

Dog handlers trained a diverse assortment of dogs to seek scarce samples on a landscape by motivating them with the promise of a reward for their successes. Typically, this worked with dogs that had a strong "ball drive"—they loved to play with a ball. These dogs worked all day to find biological samples, typically feces, in return for a few minutes of ball play for each find. The dogs learned to seek only the scat of a specific species and ignore all others. The best dogs even learned to periodically ignore the feces of a former target species and focus on another. Scat detection dogs have even learned to find floating whale feces. A dog in the bow of a boat serves as a compass needle of sorts, directing the boat operator to go in the direction the dog's sense of smell tells it the sample is located. Sophisticated analyses can now be done with DNA-laden samples collected using the simplest of low-tech field tools—a dog.

One important change that influenced wildlife research over the last few decades did not happen inside the profession but rather in the world around it. Early on, the customers of wildlife biologists were agencies that managed landscapes, the animals on them, and hunters. But in the United States, wildlife is a public trust—owned to some degree by all of us. For many years before and after World War II, the public was not well-engaged in the dialogue about wildlife conservation and management. There was not much effort to include the public interest, nor did wildlife professionals prioritize communication with the broader public. But that changed. And that could be a whole other book.

I became convinced during my career that people care a lot about wildlife. Most people I met, on learning what my profession was, wanted to share a few strongly held opinions. With time, the broader public has become much more well-informed about wildlife and the processes that affect wildlife populations. They have similarly become interested in policies that affect wildlife and the environment.

The customer base has grown—and not just a little. Sustainable policies now must address more than the desires of hunters, scientists, and agency bureaucrats. At times, this has not felt like a good thing to wildlife professionals; ultimately, I believe, it is. My profession has increasingly come to understand the importance of accounting for different perspectives about wildlife, as daunting a task as that may be. Yes, people interested in wildlife have diverse ideas and values, and those sometimes conflict with each other. But the more people care about and advocate for wildlife, the more likely we are to have durable conservation policies.

Chapter 12

It Takes a Conservation Village

As Jess touched the helicopter down on the cobblestone along the shoreline of the South Fork Nooksack River, I could see the sedated elk—dart in her rump—lying just inside the alder stand twenty yards away. I unfastened my harness tether and slid out of the doorless back seat. Chris Danilson—my mugger that day—exited right behind me. Chris was a biologist with the Sauk-Suiattle Indian Tribe. As we walked toward our sleeping elk, Jess lifted off and sped away to retrieve our crew from where we'd handled our previous elk fifteen minutes earlier.

Five minutes later, as Chris and I blindfolded the sedated elk and were checking her vitals, we heard the roar of the turbine as Jess came around the riverbend and settled onto the gravel bar again. The remaining three members of our crew hopped out and headed our way—wildlife veterinarian Joe Gaydos, associated with the University of California, Davis; Chris Madsen, biologist with the Northwest Indian Fisheries Commission; and Jennifer Ringo, WDFW biologist. Counting Jess, our elk capture team of six worked for five different employers, but we were a team, depending on each other and all working closely together on the same research goals that day.

The cultural axiom, "It takes a village," was originally coined to reflect the importance of a network of influential relationships on the healthy development of a child. The phrase has since become more generally applied to any collaborative effort to achieve a worthwhile outcome. Certainly, the work of biologists, particularly related to conservation or management outcomes, is best accomplished by broad collaborations—more resources, more skilled partners and perspectives, various stakeholders—a conservation village.

In my wildlife career, I worked for three distinctly different organizations—a federal government contractor (Battelle), a Native American wildlife program (Yakama Nation), and a state wildlife agency (WDFW). Each had its own core mission and identity. All had bright, diverse staff who were passionate about the work, pursued science-based resource management, valued conservation, and espoused the proper application of the scientific method. I never worked directly for the federal government, but in my years of research, I partnered many times with federal biologists from the Forest Service, Park Service, Fish and Wildlife Service, Bureau of Indian Affairs, and US Geological Survey.

It doesn't necessarily take a lot of people to do the mechanics of useful wildlife field research. One person does most graduate student projects—the student—sometimes with the help of a technician or two. Most of my master's degree project field work on Arid Lands elk was done by me alone, following elk around every day. I accomplished my doctoral work mostly with the help of a single technician. But there is usually synergy in collaboration—the outcome is greater than the sum of its parts. There are obvious benefits—collaborative funding, for one; and teams of people with different specialized and complementary skills, for another. Partners and stakeholders mean more people invested in the researcher's success.

Perhaps most importantly, wild animals are part of a system, both complex and usually broad in scale. The system includes other organisms, a heterogenous mosaic of potential habitat that varies in value to the animal, dynamic abiotic forces such as weather, and even human influences. Each animal population defines the scale of a study area by their daily and seasonal movements, whether they are migratory or resident, territorial or social, ecologically flexible or specialized.

The real-world relevance of this system's complexity is that effective conservation—addressing animal population viability, community dynamics, and habitat condition and trend—typically must occur at a scale beyond the ownership of a single management entity. That means research must also contemplate that scale. A single Yellowstone grizzly—let alone the entire population—may use several national forests, two national parks, state lands in three states, federal land managed by the Bureau of Land Management, and some private lands. Similarly, a single elk population in western Washington may use national forest lands, state forest lands, private commercial timberlands, WDFW lands, and private lands.

Technology now makes it possible to track the movements of even wide-ranging animals; and remotely sensed imagery—such as from satellites—also can give a researcher broadscale, albeit coarse, habitat data. Droves of data are now available to a wildlife researcher with little effort, but tools such as these, which make a big world smaller, do not negate the synergistic value of research and resource management collaboration.

Usually, no single entity holds the sole authority and responsibility for managing wildlife populations and the habitats they depend on. With a few exceptions, wildlife management authority is exercised by state wildlife agencies—stemming from the long-standing state ownership of wildlife doctrine—but federal agencies exercise wildlife management authority in national parks and over species covered by federal regulations or international treaties, such as federally listed threatened and endangered species, marine mammals, and migratory birds. And tribal sovereign nations usually have primary wildlife management authority on reservations.

Although state wildlife agencies are largely responsible for managing and conserving the animals within a state's borders, other agencies manage most of the public land that the same wildlife depends upon for habitat. In Washington—where I spent most of my career—the Department of Fish and Wildlife manages about 1 million acres of wildlife habitat, and federal agencies are the stewards of more than 12 million acres of habitat. Similarly, in Montana, where my career began, the state manages almost 7 million acres of potential habitat, while federal agencies manage more than 27 million acres. Two federal agencies manage the bulk of federal lands in the United States that support wildlife—the US Forest Service manages about 193 million acres, and the Bureau of Land Management is responsible for about 245 million acres. I learned quickly that doing field research on wild animals that traversed and drew sustenance from land managed by different entities required partnerships, clear communication, and coordination—at least, success and impact were more likely with this approach.

Collaboration was a strong element in most of the research projects I led, irrespective of my employer. The success of the Klickitat deer work, my doctoral research, and elk projects I led for WDFW in the Nooksack, Blue Mountains, Mount St. Helens, and Colockum regions, and in the Yakima herd range all depended on partnering with others. I am particularly proud of the successful state-tribal coordination we accomplished in the Klickitat deer work and with our elk work in the Nooksack. Historically, state and tribal programs worked awkwardly together at times because of past tensions and mistrust. That has improved a great deal, and I think these two projects are model examples that contributed to better working relationships.

In the Klickitat, I was the tribal research lead; and in the Nooksack, I was the state's research lead. Our success was enhanced by considerable effort to maintain effective communication, identify mutually beneficial goals, and adhere to an undying commitment of mutual respect. As the lead researcher, I also emphasized that our focus was on doing high-caliber wildlife research, not on achieving any policy agenda. That singular focus on doing good science fostered trust.

At other times, I collaborated on research I was not directing. For several years, I was on a team working to revise elk monitoring protocols in Olympic and Mount Rainier National Parks. Federal biologists of the National Park Service and US Geological Survey led this work. I also had the opportunity to be part of a multistate group of researchers known as the Western Elk Research Collaborative (WERC). In the WERC effort, elk scientists from most of the western United States contributed datasets from each state's work toward meta-analysis to better understand the broadscale drivers of juvenile elk survival and post-winter juvenile to adult female ratios.

The community approach to conducting and applying wildlife research has become increasingly common. It had to. Altogether, the interjurisdictional reality of wildlife management, the increasing complexity of research questions, the often broad scope of intended inference, and the diversity of potential stakeholders make it more likely that success will require a team of cooperators and a shared vision.

A few years back, I participated in a collaborative effort to better understand the interactions of elk nutrition, habitat influences on nutrition, and effects on elk productivity and survival. My colleagues John and Rachel Cook designed and led the effort. The Cooks had previously done good, innovative work with tame elk and controlled diets. They had developed excellent protocols for quantifying elk condition—actual body fat levels—in the field with live elk. They now wanted to apply those methods to wild elk across a broad multistate area of the West—scaling up the basic questions.

At the time, a number of elk researchers were doing field studies with elk that required capturing and collaring them—me included. So, a partnership was crafted where the Cooks would be part of each researcher's capture team. They would collect the data they needed, and each researcher would benefit by the information about local elk nutrition and habitat that their analyses would reveal.

This all took several years. I spent a lot of time in the field with John and Rachel on several separate studies I was doing with elk herds in Washington—Yakima, Colockum, and Mount St. Helens. Earlier data came from work already done in the Nooksack and on the ALE Reserve at Hanford. John and Rachel did the data analyses and wrote a nice manuscript. But their dataset was the result of collaborating with elk researchers across the West. In 2013, the Wildlife Society published the work as a *Wildlife Monograph*. The authorship list had nineteen names, including mine. All the authors contributed something that made the work better, but none of it would have happened without John and Rachel orchestrating the necessary collaboration.

The work of a naturalist is easily done alone. Even a research biologist can apply field methods working solo. That can be fun, and there have been times when my insights grew as I spent time alone among the animals I was studying. But the scientific world is ever more complicated, so achieving complex research goals and gaining support for meaningful applications of wildlife research is best done in community. Alliances can be a powerful way to do wildlife science. Sometimes it really does take a village.

Acknowledgments

I suppose there are entirely self-made people who achieve success based solely on their own intellect, work ethic, and innate abilities. I suspect they are rare. I wouldn't deceive anyone by claiming my success was all mine. Of course, I worked hard and had some useful talents. I was successful in achieving many of my goals. But I am keenly aware that others played a vital role in all my accomplishments. Many people intersected my path who had the opportunity to lend me a hand or share their wisdom, and they did. I am humbly grateful to them.

Les Pengelly was director of the Wildlife Biology Program at the University of Montana when I arrived in fall 1979. He taught one of the first classes required of us—"Survey of Wildlife Careers." Several guest lecturers were featured, and one—from the US Forest Service—told us during his visit to look around the class. "Most of you," he opined, "will never work in the wildlife field… there simply are not that many jobs." What? I scheduled an appointment with Dr. Pengelley that same week and asked him if I was wasting my time. Was this career path a realistic goal? He looked at me quietly at first and then told me that if I worked hard, and especially if I pursued a graduate degree, he was confident I could succeed. He urged me to stay the course. He was not formally my advisor, but from that day on he served willingly in that role.

We had many conversations, and he motivated me to do my best. We became friends over the next couple years, but I always referred to him as Dr. Pengelly. He encouraged me, challenged me, acknowledged my classroom successes, and eventually wrote me a key recommendation letter for graduate school. He was instrumental in my receiving the Outstanding Senior award in 1982, just before I graduated. I have never forgotten what Les did for me, how he believed in me and taught me to believe in myself, and how I might never have become a wildlife biologist without his encouragement.

I arrived at the University of Washington in fall 1982 to begin a master's degree program in wildlife biology. My major professor was Richard "Dick" Taber. A friend of Les Pengelly's, Dr. Taber was a highly regarded professor and a well-published scientist. When he died in 2016, Dick was the last surviving graduate student of Aldo Leopold, considered by many to be the father of modern wildlife conservation. I learned a great deal from Dick Taber, and he also became a longtime mentor and friend.

During my time as a graduate researcher under Dick, I often pursued questions in my work that he suggested. Each time I told Dick what I had learned about something, he acknowledged my progress and then asked me, "But what about…?" Each question answered led to a new and deeper question. Dick taught me to never stop asking questions, to always pursue a deeper understanding. I obtained my degree in 1985, but because of Dick Taber's influence, I never stopped learning. He made me a better scientist.

During my years at the University of Montana pursuing a bachelor of science degree and later a doctorate, I also grew through the significant influence of professors Chuck Jonkel, Phil Wright, Bart O'Gara, Les Marcum, Dan Pletscher, and Jack Ward Thomas. At the University of Washington, Ken Raedeke was a mentor.

Early on, I learned a great deal about field research from Lester Eberhardt. A staff wildlife researcher with PNL at Hanford during my graduate student elk study on the Arid Lands Ecology Reserve, Les became a good friend. He was tragically taken from our profession way too early. Bill Rickard, a PNL ecologist, was instrumental in creating my opportunity at Hanford. Other PNL ecologists also aided my work, particularly Lee Rogers and Richard "Dick" Fitzner.

Bill Bradley, at the time director of the Yakama Nation Wildlife Program, gave me my first long-term research job, for which I am grateful. Bill always supported my work for the Yakamas, trusted me, and was instrumental in my return to graduate school for a doctorate. My skills and maturity grew a great deal during my time working for the Yakama Nation. The work I led for the Yakamas would not have been as successful without the contributions of several tribal wildlife technicians, including Mudd Walker, Frances Bushman, John Carl, Bing Olney, Vic Ganuelas, Vern Smartlowit, and Dave Blodgett Jr. Dave deserves special thanks for being the primary technician on multiyear elk and bear research we did together on the Yakama Reservation. Dependable and incredibly skilled, he was a partner in that work.

My next big opportunity came when I joined WDFW in 2001. That move would never have happened without the support of then Wildlife Program Director Dave Brittell and Deputy Director Steve Pozzanghera. Dave recruited me to apply for an open research position; his and Steve's support never waned. Jerry Nelson was the hiring manager for that first WDFW job, and he was a tireless supporter of the work we did in the agency's Deer and Elk Section. Jerry became a good friend, and I am grateful for his trust, confidence, and support over the years.

In my research position with WDFW, my role was to lead ungulate research projects across the state. That working model required me to depend at times on local district wildlife biologists, assistant district wildlife biologists, wildlife area managers and assistant managers, and wildlife enforcement officers. There were so many contributors that I fear if I tried to name them all, I'd unintentionally leave someone out. They all made important contributions, for which I am grateful, and they all deserve credit for our joint success. Because I worked closely on multiple projects with Will Moore, Paul Wik, and Annemarie Prince, I want to thank them especially. I also want to thank retired WDFW biologist Pat Miller, who intersected my journey multiple times over a span of about thirty years. Pat and I worked together on Klickitat deer and Mount St. Helens elk—both major efforts for me. Dan Morrison was also key to the success of the Klickitat deer work. We had different employers, but we were an effective and productive team. I also owe gratitude to WDFW wildlife veterinarians Briggs Hall and Kristin Mansfield for their close collaboration on wildlife captures for our research. They were amicable and capable partners, and they taught me a great deal.

These are the people I crossed paths with academically and professionally. They helped me grow and achieve success in my career. But none of it would have been possible, and so enjoyable, without the most important people in my life—my family. My wife Kim has been a constant supporter and partner in all life's most important decisions.

She was even, briefly, my field assistant. Kim encouraged me to stretch for things that were not going to be easy, like this book. I love her and owe her much, and I am so thankful we have made this journey together. Our children—Andy, Kyle, and Katie—also supported their dad. They incurred impacts, such as having to leave home for a year and live in Missoula while I did my doctoral coursework, and they never complained. The times when I got to observe the natural world with them and show them the work I did to conserve it added so much to this adventure. Our shared days in the field are my best memories.

Index

Note: References in italic refer to figures

About the Author

Scott McCorquodale spent forty years as a professional wildlife biologist, beginning in Montana and then working extensively in his current home state of Washington. He has a bachelor of science degree and doctorate from the University of Montana and a master of science degree from the University of Washington. He carried out field research on grizzly and black bears, mule deer, black-tailed deer, Rocky Mountain and Roosevelt elk, moose, and other large mammals. He worked both in government agency and Native American wildlife program contexts.

Over the course of his career, he published more than twenty-five peer-reviewed scientific papers, several book chapters, numerous agency reports, and a handful of popular magazine articles. He also served twenty years on the Board of Associate Editors of the *Journal of Wildlife Management*.

His research took him to every part of Washington, and his field work included extensive time flying in helicopters and small planes. He became a skilled helicopter darter, darting over a thousand animals during his career.

A recipient of the Washington Department of Fish and Wildlife's Director's Award and Best Science Award for his contributions to wildlife conservation and management, McCorquodale is recognized statewide and nationally for his contributions as a leader in the wildlife profession.